FLORIDA

A HISTORY IN PICTURES

Mike McGinness • Jeff Davies

MacIntyre Purcell Publishing Inc.
Lunenburg, Nova Scotia

MacIntyre Purcell Publishing Inc.
232 Fairmont Road
Cloverville, Nova Scotia
B2G 2K9
(902) 640-3350
www.macintyrepurcell.com
info@macintyrepurcell.com

Printed and bound in China.

Cover design: Gwen North
Book design: Gwen North

Cover photo: Children and adults at Venetian Pool, Coral Gables, 1930s. As George Merrick went about creating Coral Gables, a city with Mediterranean features such as grand entrances, plazas, and Mediterranean-style homes, the limestone being used to create the buildings was taken from a quarry pit. This quarry became Venetian Pool, which was opened in 1924 as the Venetian Casino. The pool was transformed into a paradise, and it was quite a destination for the high society people of the day. Movie stars Johnny Weissmuller and Esther Williams both appeared there to large crowds. The pool is included in the National Register of Historic Places, the only swimming pool to have such a designation.
Photo courtesy of Coral Gables Memory.

ISBN: 978-1-77276-172-6

Library and Archives Canada Cataloguing in Publication

Title: Florida : a history in pictures / Mike McGinness and Jeff Davies
Names: McGinness, Mike, author. | Davies, Jeff (Author of Florida), author.
Identifiers: Canadiana 20220204144 | ISBN 9781772761726 (hardcover)
Subjects: LCSH: Florida—History—Pictorial works. | LCGFT: Illustrated works.
Classification: LCC F312 .M34 2022 | DDC 975.90022/2—dc23

A FLORIDA TIMELINE

12,000 to 10,000 BC: Habitation by the first humans in Florida. These early Paleo-Indian or Paleo-Americans were descendants of the primitive hunters and gatherers that crossed the Bering Strait from Asia. More than likely, Florida was one of the last places in the Americas they settled.

5,000 BC: The Paleo-Indian culture evolved into the Archaic culture. Permanent settlements were established, primarily on the coast, and were dependent upon shellfish and plant gathering.

500 AD: Woodland culture emerged with year-round settlements, reliance on hunting small animals, and the development of farming.

700 AD: Beginning of tribes and chiefdoms: various tribes included Ais, Apalachee, Calusa, Jeaga, Mayaimi, Tequesta, Timucua, and Tocobaga.

1513: The first Europeans made landfall. Spanish explorer Juan Ponce de León's expedition landed on the east coast near present-day St. Augustine. He named the peninsula Florida as the season was Pascua Florida (Flowery Easter). He encountered Native Americans.

1539: Hernando de Soto landed with an 800-man expedition near Tampa Bay. He explored central and northern Florida on his way to the Mississippi River.

1540s: Diseases introduced by Europeans began to decimate the Native Americans. Within a century, 90 percent of the population perished.

1559: Spanish explorer Tristán de Luna y Arellano established the earliest multi-year European colony in the continental United States at present day Pensacola.

1562: French Explorer Jean Ribault landed near St. Augustine and began an attempt to colonize the area and drive out the Spanish.

1564: Led by René Goulaine de Laudonnière, the French established Fort Caroline near the mouth of the St. Johns River at present day Jacksonville.

1565: Spain's Pedro Menéndez de Avilés established St. Augustine; Spanish troops expelled the French from Florida.

1586: Englishman Sir Francis Drake and his fleet of 23 ships attacked and pillaged St. Augustine.

1596: The Franciscans took over the Spanish missions in an effort to spread Catholicism. They eventually established over 100 missions in Florida and Georgia.

1603: A mission chain was founded along the east coast and into the mainland toward Apalachee territory.

1656: The Timucua rebelled against Spanish authority after suffering huge losses due to Spanish invasion, slave labor, and disease. Timucua chief Lucas Menéndez called for a rebellion and killed all soldiers and civilians at the San Pedro y San Pablo de Patale Mission near present day Tallahassee. Mission San Luis de Apalachee was established at Tallahassee and functioned as the capital of the western missions in Florida from 1656 to 1704. It was populated by more than 1,500 residents.

Ponce de León. *Photo courtesy of Wikimedia Commons.*

1668: English privateer Robert Searle launched an attack on St. Augustine that destroyed much of the city. He stole valuables, held daughters of wealthy families for ransom, and seized African and Native Americans to sell into slavery.

1672: Citing the need to protect the city from further attacks, the Spanish, with the help of labor from slaves and Indigenous peoples, began constructing Castillo de San Marcos at St. Augustine.

1698: The Spanish re-established Pensacola, a settlement first established in 1559 and abandoned two years later due to a hurricane.

1702-1704: English and Spanish fought for control of Florida. The English destroyed Spanish missions.

1738–1740: Fort Mose was established by the Spanish a few miles north of St. Augustine as a refuge for freed African Americans. They were considered "free" as long as they accepted Catholicism, were baptized with Christian names, and agreed to be a part of the Spanish colonial militia.

1763: The Spanish transferred Florida to the English in exchange for Havana, Cuba, which the British had captured from Spain during the Seven Years War (1756-63). The Spanish left Florida after the exchange. The colony was divided into East and West Florida. The British expanded agriculture, especially cotton, rice, and indigo. St. Augustine remained the capital of East Florida, with Pensacola the capital of West Florida. James Grant was appointed Governor of British Florida.

1768: The British colony of New Smyrna was established by Dr. Andrew Turnbull. It was the largest attempt at British colonization in the New World.

Tampa Bay Hotel.
Photo courtesy of Detroit Publishing Company.

1783: Florida was returned to Spain again following the signing of the Treaty of Paris, signaling the end of the American Revolutionary War.

1814: Andrew Jackson invaded Florida in pursuit of runaway slaves and members of the Seminole Tribe, thus starting the First Seminole War. U.S. settlers, Spanish citizens, British agents, and people of the Creek Nation clashed in West Florida. Jackson, ignoring the international border, burned Native American villages, hanged two British subjects, and captured St. Marks and Pensacola.

1819: The Adams-Onis Treaty was signed between Spain and the United States. Control of Florida was ceded to the United States in exchange for settling a boundary dispute along the Sabine River in Spanish Texas, and five million dollars.

1821: Florida became a U.S. Territory. Andrew Jackson was appointed Governor and returned to establish a new territorial government on behalf of the United States.

1824: Tallahassee was chosen as the capital because of its location midway between Pensacola and St. Augustine.

1845: Florida gained statehood and was admitted to the Union as the 27th U.S. state.

1856–1858: The Third Seminole War ceased; many Native Americans perished in the conflicts and most that remained were forced out of Florida.

1861: The Civil War began. Florida seceded from the Union and joined the Confederacy.

1865: The Civil War ended. Florida was under Federal control. Slavery ended. Emancipation Day was celebrated on May 12. Reconstruction began. Major settlement of north Florida took place during this period as families from war-torn Georgia, Alabama, South Carolina, and elsewhere moved to the state.

1868: Florida was readmitted to the Union with a new state constitution guaranteeing civil rights and giving African Americans the right to vote.

1880s: Settlers flocked to Florida. New industries were developed and existing ones were expanded, including major railroads, citrus production and exportation, phosphate mining, timber, cattle exportation, farming, and tourism.

1883: Henry B. Plant's South Florida Railroad became the first railroad to arrive in Tampa.

1887: The town of Eatonville, six miles north of Orlando, became the first incorporated municipality in America governed by African Americans.

1888: Henry Flagler's Ponce de León Hotel opened in St. Augustine.

1891: Henry B. Plant's Tampa Bay Hotel opened in Tampa.

1894–1895: The Great Freeze hit Florida and destroyed much of the citrus crop.

1896: Henry Flagler's Florida East Coast Railway reached Miami.

1898: Florida played an important role in the Spanish-American War. The Plant System of railways transported troops to Florida and Plant Line steamships carried troops and supplies to Cuba. The Tampa Bay Hotel became the headquarters for the U.S. Army officers awaiting the order to embark. Lieutenant Colonel Theodore Roosevelt and the Rough Riders trained in the camps near the Hotel. Embarkment camps were also established in Miami and Jacksonville.

1901: Jacksonville was devastated by the Great Fire of 1901. It was one of the worst disasters in Florida history and the third largest urban fire in the U.S., next to the Great Chicago Fire of 1871 and the 1906 San Francisco fire.

1905: The Buckman Act was passed that reorganized the existing six Florida colleges into three institutions, segregated by race and gender.

1905: Work began on Henry Flagler's Over-Sea Railroad which would connect Miami and Key West.

1906: A powerful hurricane hit the Keys, killing 240 people, including 135 workers of the Over-Sea Railroad. The storm continued northeast and slammed Miami, destroying structures with high winds and causing major flooding. Other towns and cities along the east coast were impacted as well.

1912: Henry Flagler arrived aboard the first train into Key West, which marked the completion of the Florida East Coast (FEC) Railway's Over-Sea Railroad. This linked the entire east coast of Florida, from Jacksonville to Key West, by a single railroad system. The project was so ambitious it was dubbed by many the "Eighth Wonder of the World."

1920s: Florida experienced massive growth and many new towns emerged. The Florida land boom shaped Florida's future for decades to come.

1926: The Great Miami Hurricane devastated the Miami area. As a result, the land boom in Florida ended. The hurricane represented an early start to the Great Depression for Floridians. The death toll was estimated to be 325 to 800 people.

1928: Major advances in transportation occurred. The Over-Sea Highway opened for vehicles, connecting Key West to mainland Florida, and the Tamiami Trail opened to traffic linking Tampa and Miami. Another massive hurricane struck Florida and made landfall near West Palm Beach. The most severe effects were felt around Lake Okeechobee where flooding killed as many as 2,500 people. Damage was estimated at $25 million.

1929: The Great Depression began. Floridians were already reeling from two recent hurricanes and the 1926 burst of the economic bubble when money and credit ran out, and banks and investors abruptly stopped trusting the paper millionaires. Another blow was dealt to Florida when one of the world's most destructive pests, the Mediterranean fruit fly, was detected near Orlando, crippling the citrus industry. Quarantine was established, and troops set up roadblocks and checkpoints to search vehicles for any contraband citrus fruit. Florida's citrus production was cut by about 60 percent.

1931: In an effort to revitalize the economy, the Florida legislature passed a law allowing pari-mutuel betting on horse and dog racing. Slot machines and Jai-alai were added in 1935.

1933: Franklin D. Roosevelt was elected President of the United States. He introduced his New Deal, and promised to get the country and people back on their feet. Soon, millions of Americans were working again. One of the programs of the New Deal was called the Civilian Conservation Corps, or CCC. Young men from all over the country lived in work camps. About 40,000 Floridians participated in the CCC. They received food and clothing and their paychecks were sent home to their families. Some of the work in Florida consisted

Over-Sea Railroad.
Photo courtesy of Library of Congress.

of cutting down millions of trees to build fire lines, planting 13 million trees, and creating state parks and wildlife preserves.

1935: The Works Progress Administration (later renamed Work Projects Administration), or WPA was introduced. As part of Roosevelt's New Deal initiative, the program was designed to put people to work by improving public infrastructure, including parks, schools, and roads. Most of the jobs were in construction. Florida benefited greatly by this program. In September 1935 the Labor Day Hurricane struck the Keys killing 408 people. It remains the strongest hurricane ever to make landfall in the United States.

1938: Reconstruction of parts of the Over-Sea Railroad, originally built by Henry Flagler, was completed by the Civilian Conservation Corps. Parts of the track had been heavily damaged during the 1935 Labor Day Hurricane. Reopening the railroad once again linked Miami to Key West and helped bring tourism back to the Keys.

Apollo 11. *Photo courtesy of NASA.gov*

1939-1945: World War II impacted Florida greatly. The warm climate and the abundance of vacant land were ideal for the building of military bases and for training soldiers. A total of 172 various military installations were established. The war effort sent large amounts of money into Florida, leading to growth after the Great Depression. War contracts helped to rebuild Florida's manufacturing, agricultural, and tourism businesses.

1946: (March 17) Jackie Robinson took the field in Daytona Beach for the Montreal Royals, the Class AAA International League affiliate of the Brooklyn Dodgers. The spring training game against the Dodgers was Robinson's first appearance as a member of the Dodgers organization, and the first time an African American player played for a minor league team against a major league team since the color line was implemented in baseball in the 1880s. A few weeks later, on April 7, Sanford police chief Roy G. Williams ordered Jackie Robinson removed from a minor league game in that city for violating racist Jim Crow policies by joining the field with white players. The park was later named in honor of the longtime sheriff. In 1997, the City of Sanford issued a public apology, and in 2020, the Sanford City Commission voted unanimously to change the name from Roy G. Williams Park to Elliott Avenue Park.

1949: President Harry S. Truman signed Public Law 60 which established the Joint Long Range Proving Ground at Cape Canaveral, the precursor to the space program.

1954: The U.S. Supreme Court ruled in the *Brown v. Board of Education* case that school segregation was unconstitutional. Many in the State of Florida resisted the decision, prolonging desegregation until the early seventies.

1959: Fidel Castro assumed power in Cuba which resulted in an influx of Cuban immigrants to Florida.

1960: A racially motivated attack dubbed Ax Handle Saturday occurred in Hemming Park in Jacksonville. Approximately 200 Ku Klux Klan members attacked Civil Rights protesters with baseball bats and ax handles. Police initially did not intervene in the attacks and only got involved when members of an African American group called the Boomerangs and other African Americans came to the defense of the protesters. Most arrested were those trying to stop the attacks.

1961: Alan B. Shepard, Jr. became the first American in space during a suborbital flight aboard his Mercury capsule named Freedom 7. President John F. Kennedy committed the United States to achieving a lunar landing before the end of the decade.

1963: President John F. Kennedy made several stops in Florida, including Miami, Tampa, and Cape Canaveral, days before his November 22 assassination in Dallas, Texas.

1968: The Republican National Convention was held at the Miami Beach Convention Center.

1969: Apollo 11 was launched from Cape Kennedy on July 16, carrying Commander Neil Armstrong, Command Module Pilot Michael Collins, and Lunar Module Pilot Edwin "Buzz" Aldrin. The objective of Apollo 11 was to complete a national goal set by President John F. Kennedy on May 25, 1961: perform a crewed lunar landing and return to Earth. An estimated 650 million people watched Armstrong's televised image and heard his voice describe the event as he took "...one small step for a man, one giant leap for mankind" on July 20. On July 24, the astronauts safely splashed down in the Pacific Ocean, completing their mission.

1971: Walt Disney World opened and changed the landscape of Florida tourism and the economy of the state.

1972: The Democratic and Republican National Conventions were held at the Miami Beach Convention Center. The Miami Dolphins dominated the National Football League, winning every game they played, including the Super Bowl.

1980: Amidst an economic downturn in Cuba and an increasing number of dissident Cubans seeking asylum, Fidel Castro announced on April 20th that all Cubans wishing to emigrate to the U.S. were free to board boats at the port of Mariel west of Havana, and leave. Between April and October 1980, some 1,700 boats carried 125,000 Cubans to Florida. Many of them were released from prisons and mental institutions. An estimated 25,000 Haitians also arrived during this period.

1981: A new era in spaceflight began. NASA launched its first crewed Space Shuttle, Columbia, on April 12 for a two-day mission piloted by Orlandoan John Young, and Robert Crippen.

1985: The Spanish treasure galleon *Nuestra Señora de Atocha,* which sank off of the Florida Keys during a hurricane in 1622, was found by treasure hunter Mel Fisher and his team of salvagers. The State of Florida claimed title to the wreck and legal battles ensued. Eight years later, the U.S. Supreme Court ruled in favor of the treasure hunters. The wreck of the *Nuestra Señora de Atocha* is considered the most valuable shipwreck ever recovered.

1986: On January 28, the space shuttle Challenger exploded 73 seconds after liftoff, killing all seven crew members on board and changing NASA's space program forever. The disaster occurred during Challenger's 10th launch from Kennedy Space Center.

1992: Hurricane Andrew, a massive Category 5 storm, made landfall in south Florida at Homestead. At the time, it was the most costly natural disaster in the history of the U.S., not to be surpassed until Hurricane Katrina 13 years later.

1994: After rioting in Cuba, 35,000 Cubans came to Florida aboard boats and makeshift rafts. Fearing a major exodus,

the Clinton administration mandated that all rafters captured at sea be detained at the Guantanamo Bay Naval Base. Those who made it to shore were allowed to pursue residency. Eventually, the Clinton administration announced that the majority of the detainees would be processed and allowed to immigrate.

1998: During the summer months, wildfires, sparked mostly by lightning strikes, brought severe damage to the state. Blazes crossed natural firebreaks such as rivers and interstate highways. Firefighters from across the country responded in an unprecedented suppression response. Regular activities such as Fourth of July celebrations, sporting events, tourism, and daily life were profoundly interrupted for millions of residents and visitors in the northeastern part of the state.

2000: Disputed Florida ballots in the United States presidential election delayed the results of the overall national result.

2004: Four hurricanes (Charley, Frances, Ivan, and Jeanne) struck Florida in a span of six weeks causing extensive damage and killing at least 19.

2014: Florida surpassed New York in population and became the third most populous state in the U.S.

2016: Tragedy unfolded in Orlando as a lone gunman entered the Pulse nightclub, and in a senseless act of hate, took 49 lives in the deadliest mass shooting in modern American history, only to be surpassed a year later by another mass shooting in Las Vegas. The site currently serves as a memorial to the lives lost, with a more permanent memorial still in the development stages.

2018: Another mass shooting occurred in Marjory Stoneman Douglas High School in the south Florida town of Parkland. In total, 17 lives were lost in the deadliest high school shooting in American history. The shooting came at a period of heightened public support for stricter gun control laws.

2020: On March 1, Florida officially reported its first two COVID-19 cases, in Manatee and Hillsborough counties. However, evidence suggested that community spread of the virus began in Florida as early as the first week of January.

2021: Led by Tom Brady, the Tampa Bay Buccaneers won their second Super Bowl by defeating the Kansas City Chiefs 31-9. It marked the first time a National Football League team won the championship game in their home stadium. The Los Angeles Rams repeated that accomplishment a year later. The Buccaneers won their first Super Bowl in 2002.

Buccaneers. *Photo courtesy of* Huffington Post.

FROM THE AUTHORS

Florida: A History in Pictures offers a glimpse into the history of this uniquely beautiful state. Our names are Mike McGinness and Jeff Davies. We believe we have compiled an interesting collection of historical photos that will take you on an excursion of discovery into Florida's past.

With the emergence of *Facebook* and the "groups" platform, Mike McGinness started a *Facebook* group called Historic Orlando in 2012, (since renamed Historic Orlando - The Original). Jeff Davies came along shortly after, and with the help of our dedicated group of administrators, the group quickly gained a dedicated following of like-minded people.

We then decided to expand our reach, so we started a second group called Historic Florida, (since renamed to Historic Florida - The Original). As of the time of this writing, we have nearly 200,000 members, and almost as many photos. We've been told that we are the largest Florida history group on *Facebook*. Our members are of all ages and from all walks of life, but they all have a common interest — learning more about the history of this great state.

It has been an interesting journey, to say the least, and we've learned a lot about Florida along the way. Without the participation of our wonderful members and our great team of administrators, none of this would have been possible. Our fine administrators include Vicky Griffin, Tim Jackson, Gary Barres, Nick Wynne, and last but not least, Lyn Chilton, whose fine research and attention to detail was instrumental in the creation of this project.

Creating this book has been a great experience of discovery for us and it would not have been possible without the help and support of certain people including Seth H. Bramson, Joy Wallace Dickinson, Eliot Kleinberg, John MacIntyre, Vernon Oickle, Kaitlyn Hof-Mahoney, Susan Gillis, Megan Scalian, Joanne Parandjuk, Jamie Rogers, Toasy Martin, Vale Tim Fillmon, Cynthia Tamargo, Larry Martin, Ruth Anne Witter Maloy, Carol Vallad, Jody McCreary, Donna Starratt, Bret Ribotsky, Melanie Homer, Ron Jaffe, Gary Kirkland, Bill Watson, Gordon Sims, Donna Smith, Phillip Pessar, David Renz, Mary Alice Hunt, Marjorie Shropshire, Tom Moore, Angela Mosely, Mike Olsen, Martha Morgan, Cassidy Alexander, Ashley Cusack, Doug Head, Dick Camnitz, Patti Barrett, William LaMartin, May Alice Hunt, Bill Drayton, and Susan Ryan.

We'd also like to thank those who shared photos with us that we were unable to use in this project. Also, to the various individuals and organizations we met along the way, in person or virtually, thank you so much for your time and guidance. If we've left anyone out, please accept our sincere apologies.

I've always been fiercely proud, and considered myself extremely lucky to be a Floridian. There's nowhere else I'd rather call home.

My fascination with the past was passed down to me from my father who loved reading history books. His favorite topic was probably the Civil War, but he enjoyed learning about a variety of things. As a kid, I'd leaf through his books, studying the long-forgotten faces. I'd wonder what they were thinking and what they were doing. I'd ponder about what their everyday life must have been like, and what trials and tribulations they must have gone through.

When I was young and we'd go on family vacations, my dad always made a point of stopping at historically significant places along our route. At every historical marker, he'd slow the car, and often get out and read them. When I was 12, we went on a vacation to Washington, D.C. Of course, we hit all of the monuments, the Smithsonian Museum, the U.S. Capitol Building, and other landmarks.

I remember standing in the center of the Capitol's rotunda and my dad telling me about the many important people who'd been on that very spot. I think it was at that moment that I first felt a real connection to the past that continues to this day.

I was born in Orlando in 1963. I've lived in Central Florida my entire life, with the exception of five years in Tampa, and five years in Snellville, Georgia, during my childhood and teen years. These days, in addition to my history endeavors, I maintain a full-time job at a company I've worked at for the last 38 years. I also enjoy spending time with the love of my life, Robin, and I try to see my awesome kids Daniel and Ellissa as often as possible. My other interests include sports, music, animals, and anything involving nature.

—Mike McGinness

My passion for history has spanned many decades. As a young child, my great-grandmother would give me various books to read encompassing subjects from history to science. She would enclose handwritten notes about each subject and I was expected to review the book and be prepared to discuss its content as well as current events on my next visit. I believe this laid the groundwork for a lifelong interest in history and curiosity for learning.

I came to Miami Beach, Florida, via Brooklyn, New York. My family relocated to North Bay Village when I was just five years old. My parents felt Miami Beach was a fertile location to open their own television and electronics business. Mostly because I was always interested in the history behind old pictures, I became known as the family historian. Having a photographic memory for facts and dates didn't hurt either.

As I grew up, I became intrigued by older buildings and destinations. I would either ride my bike or take a bus to visit places in Metro Miami to study the historic structures. Family car trips and train rides throughout the state increased my thirst for Florida state knowledge.

I eventually became the third generation to work in the audio/video electronics business and continue with this profession today. I live in Boca Raton, Florida, and have been married for 28 years to my wife, Laurie. I have fraternal twin daughters, Allison and Stephanie, who are 24 years old.

With the emergence of *Facebook*, my friend Mike McGinness thought it would be fun to share his interest in Florida history by creating a *Facebook* group. Initially, he thought it would just be a good site for him to share photos and content but eventually, Mike realized a few of his friends might want to view it as well. We collaborated and before we knew it, we reached a milestone of 5,000 members, then 50,000 members and now close to 200,000 members who share pictures and valuable content daily.

Our members stem from all walks of life. They include scholars, teachers, students, historians, politicians, celebrities, authors, professionals, and most importantly, people who are genuinely interested in the history of Florida.

—Jeff Davies

FLORIDA: A HISTORY IN PICTURES

Quartermaster Depot, Jacksonville, 1865. *Photo courtesy of Massachusetts Historical Society.*

Jacksonville

During the Civil War, control of Jacksonville changed hands four times between the Union and the Confederate armies. This 1865 photo shows a depot established by the Union Quartermaster Department. The Quartermasters were responsible for establishing transportation networks, acquiring and procuring supplies, and getting them to the army. They provided clothing, equipment, animals, and services to keep the war effort going. This photo features members of the 54th Massachusetts Infantry Regiment, a volunteer African American unit made famous in the 1989 movie *Glory*, during their time in Jacksonville.

The City of St. Augustine has a fascinating history. For hundreds of years before Europeans arrived, Timucua occupied the area. The Timucua were a Native American people who lived in Northeast and North Central Florida and southeast Georgia. They were the largest indigenous group in that area with an estimated population of 200,000. They fished, hunted, and cultivated corn, beans, and squash. The chief of the Timucua in the St. Augustine region in 1565, when Europeans first arrived, was Seloy. His town has been located archaeologically on the grounds of what is today the Fountain of Youth Park, about one mile north of the Castillo de San Marcos. The first permanent occupation of Europeans began in 1565 when it was founded by the Spanish admiral, Pedro Menéndez de Avilés. He was given authority from the Spanish Crown to establish a permanent colony from which the Spanish treasure fleet could be defended and Spain's claimed territories in North America protected against incursions by other European powers, namely the French, who were also looking to colonize the area. In 1763, the Treaty of Paris ended the Seven Years' War. Spain ceded Florida and St. Augustine to the British in exchange for their relinquishing control of occupied Havana. Florida came under Spanish control again from 1784 to 1821. There was no new settlement, only small detachments of soldiers, as the fortifications decayed. Spain itself was the scene of war between 1808 and 1814 and had little control over Florida. In 1821, the Adams–Onís Treaty peaceably turned the Spanish provinces in Florida and, with them, St. Augustine, over to the United States.

St. Augustine

Two gentlemen leisurely sitting on chairs, one reads while the other acknowledges the photographer. They are accompanied by two young boys, while a third man sits by himself in the distance. This view is looking north on Charlotte Street, one of the most picturesque streets in the city. It has played an important part in historic and civic events over the years, although there doesn't appear to be much going on this particular day.

Charlotte Street in St. Augustine, 1875.
Photo courtesy of Flagler College Archives.

Altamonte Springs

In 1880, the South Florida Railroad completed a line from Sanford to Orlando. A flag stop was established at Snowville or Snows Station where the railroad crosses State Road 436 today. To sound more appealing to potential tourists, the community of Snowville changed its name to Altamonte Station and eventually Altamonte Springs, for various springs in the area. The horse-drawn trolley under the structure on the left transported visitors over a narrow tramway back and forth between the train station and the Altamonte Hotel. The hotel, which was built in 1882/1883, operated seasonally for 70 years before burning down in 1953.

Waiting for the train, Altamonte Springs, 1886.
Photo by Stanley J. Morrow, courtesy of the Floyd and Marion Rinhart Collection, Miami-Dade Public Library System.

FLORIDA A HISTORY IN PICTURES

Pensacola

Volunteer firemen from the Germania Steam Fire Engine and Hose Company are seen here in the 1880s. The group was formed in 1870 and was headquartered at 17 East Zaragoza Street. In 1888, the Germania Company merged with two other fire companies to form the Fire Association of Pensacola, a city-run volunteer association. Volunteers continued to be the only means of fire protection until January 1, 1888, when the city established a full-time department of paid firefighters under Chief John Baker.

Photo courtesy of the New York Public Library, additional information from the Pensacola Fire Department.

A crowd gathered at a fair in Orlando, 1880s.

Photo courtesy of Digital Public Library of America/University of Miami Libraries.

Orlando

City and county fairs in Orlando at the turn of the last century were much different from what we know today. There were the traditional exhibitions of livestock and produce such as oranges, grapefruit, celery, sweet potatoes, corn, tomatoes, beans, pecans, pumpkins, apples, jellies, and jams — all illustrative of what Florida can and does grow. There was also a gala parade of automobiles and decorated floats, representing local businesses and civic organizations. Activities included harness races, fancy roping and riding, roping steers from automobiles, a polo game for the Ladies' Cup, and riding wild bucking horses. Attendees were instructed that "if you have a wild bucking horse don't fail to bring him out."

Lake Formosa

Located just north of Orlando, the Lake Formosa area was settled in 1880 by an attorney from Pennsylvania named James M. Wilcox. He purchased 40 acres and built the West End Hotel. In 1881, the South Florida Railroad came to the area and established a stop on the west side of the tracks, near what is now Princeton St., and called it Willcox. By 1887, the Village of Willcox had grown to 125 residents and was renamed Formosa. One of the first post offices in the area was established in the general store and it remained in operation until 1907. This image shows what the area must have looked like when James Wilcox first settled here.

An 1880s or 1890s view of Lake Formosa near Orlando.
Photo courtesy of Matheson History Museum.

Casino and tennis court at the Alcazar Hotel in St. Augustine, 1891.
Photo courtesy of Floyd and Marion Rinhart Collection, University of Miami Library; additional information from the Lightner Museum.

St. Augustine

The Alcazar Hotel was built in 1888 by railroad magnate Henry Flagler, and was his second grand hotel in St. Augustine, the first being the Ponce de Leon Hotel. The Alcazar was initially conceived as an entertainment annex for the Ponce de Leon, but the design was soon revised and expanded to create an independent hotel. Architects John Merven Carrère and Thomas Hastings drew inspiration from Spanish architecture, enriching the building with elements of Italian Renaissance and Moorish design. The Alcazar closed during the depression in 1931. In 1947, the hotel was purchased by Otto Lightner and was transformed into the Lightner Museum.

Dade City

These members of the Masonic Lodge from Mt. Zion met in Dade City, 1892. They were responsible for establishing another Masonic lodge in Dade City as well as one in Trilby. Parts of the Trilby building were moved by horse and rollers from Twin Lakes. Bank of Pasco County, chartered in 1889, is under construction in the left center background. This view is looking east approximately where the Seaboard Air Line tracks crossed Meridian Avenue. The temporary court house was in one of the buildings on the right.

Photo courtesy of the Helen Eck Sparkman Collection, additional information from Bill Drayton and The Florida Pioneer Museum.

Workers pick oranges in the John B. Stetson groves in DeLand, 1894.

Photo courtesy of Stetson University Library Archives.

DeLand

In 1885, the town's founder Henry DeLand convinced his friend John B. Stetson to visit Persimmon Hollow, now known as DeLand. Stetson, a hat manufacturer whose hats are commonly referred to as Stetsons, spent the next 20 winters in the blossoming town. He became an active business and community leader. DeLand Academy, which was founded in 1883, changed its name to John B. Stetson University in 1889 to honor Stetson who made generous donations to the school. John B. Stetson was a benefactor to the university and served alongside Henry A. DeLand as a founding trustee.

A gathering at the Waters S. Davis house at Cape Florida, 1895.

Photo courtesy of University of Miami Library.

Cape Florida on Key Biscayne

On the left is Ralph Middleton Munroe, a famous yacht designer and an early resident of Coconut Grove. Munroe made his living by designing yachts for many of South Florida's pioneers. He also worked as a wrecker, salvaging boats that had run aground in Biscayne Bay. Munroe founded the Biscayne Bay Yacht Club in 1887, and was the club's first commodore, a position he held for 22 years. He was an accomplished amateur photographer. Many of his photographs were used in magazines, newspapers, and books as illustrations. His photographs offer a rare glimpse of what pioneer days looked like in early Miami.

Manatee County

The steamer *Margaret* of the Plant Line ran between Ellenton (near Bradenton) and Tampa. The sign over the door of the wooden building at left reads Southern Express Company, a railroad owned by Henry B. Plant. Henry helped to develop Florida with railways, steamships, and luxury hotels. He owned railroads up and down the southeastern United States. After the Civil War, he started buying up bankrupt railroad lines. Eventually his railroads made it down through Central Florida and then crossed over to the west coast and went all the way down to Fort Myers. Plant also operated a steamship line. After bringing his railway to Tampa, Plant used his steamship line to link west Florida to Key West and Cuba. This allowed for the transportation of both goods and people via train and steamship.

Loading vegetables for shipment at the Palmetto dock in Manatee County, about 1895.

Photo courtesy of Manatee County Public Library.

The Detroit Hotel

The Detroit was built in 1888 by Peter Demens, who was also responsible for bringing the railroad to St. Petersburg. The hotel was built as the result of agreement between Demens and General John Constantine Williams. General Williams gave Demens part of his land holdings in exchange for Demens' agreement to bring the Orange Belt Railway to St. Petersburg. Local folklore claims that Demens and Williams flipped a silver half dollar to see who would claim the right to name the town. Demens won the toss and chose St. Petersburg after his hometown in Russia. Although it was not a part of the original agreement, Williams was allowed to name the hotel and chose Detroit after his birthplace. Demens built the hotel for $10,000, of which Williams contributed half. The Orange Belt Railway started offering tours to St. Petersburg in 1889, and advertisements began to appear in northern papers featuring the Detroit Hotel and

The Detroit Hotel, St. Petersburg, 1890s.
Photo courtesy of PICRYL, additional information from St. Pete Blogspot, *Library of Congress.*

the healthful St. Petersburg climate, bringing early tourism to town. In the late 1890s a gazebo with a minaret was constructed, and around 1910, a brick addition with 63 rooms was added on the west side of the building. The year 1914 saw another brick addition on the east side. With that expansion, the original wood structure was encased by the brick. A big hurricane struck the west coast of Florida in 1921, damaging many of the buildings and houses in St. Petersburg. The Detroit lost part of its roof in the storm, but the hotel remained in business and it was not long before the damage had been repaired. The Detroit closed as a hotel in 1993. In 2002, it was converted to condos, and is today a four-story building.

Archer

Archer is a small town about 15 miles southwest of Gainesville. Archer started in the 1840s as a frontier village named Deer Hammock or Darden's Hammock. Early settlers lived in small cabins and grew fruits and vegetables and hunted for their food. Their drinking water was supplied from a sinkhole in the area. The Florida Railroad reached the village in 1858, which shifted the site of the town eastward. At this point, the city was renamed Archer, after James T. Archer, Florida's first Secretary of State. The first trains stopped in Archer in 1859. Notable residents over the years include Thomas Gilbert Pearson (1873–1943), a founder of the National Association of Audubon Societies which became the National Audubon Society, and early rock and roll legend Ellas Bates (1928-2008), more commonly known by his stage name Bo Diddley.

A man proudly showing off a stalk of bananas grown in Archer, 1890s.
Photo courtesy of Matheson History Museum.

The Central City Giants, 1890s, Gainesville. *Photo courtesy of Matheson History Museum.*

Central City Giants

The Giants, also known as the Central City Nine, were Gainesville's African American team. The city also had an all-white team known as the Oak Halls. Both teams played against outside competition at what was known locally as the Ballpark, which was located at Porters Quarters.

Stetson University President John Forbes stands with an umbrella in front of DeLand Hall with a group of students in 1890.

Photo courtesy of Stetson University Library Archives.

DeLand Hall

DeLand Hall preceded the university as an elementary and high school known as DeLand Academy. It is still standing and is the oldest building in Florida continuously associated with higher education. The Academy was founded and built by Henry A. DeLand, a New Yorker, who deeded the building to the university. It opened on Oct. 13, 1884, with a construction cost of $4,000.

A diverse fishing party gigging sheepshead from a wharf on San Carlos Bay in 1907.
Photo courtesy of Florida Gulf Coast University.

San Carlos Bay

The man standing in the middle is holding the gig and more than likely is responsible for the large haul of fish. The man on the left appears to be running a hook on a line without a pole. Located southwest of Fort Myers at the mouth of the Caloosahatchee River, San Carlos Bay has long been a popular spot for fishing.

The area was once home to the Calusa (kah-loos-ah) Native American tribe. The Calusa, originally called the Calos which means "fierce people," were descendants of Paleo-Americans who inhabited Southwest Florida approximately 12,000 years ago. The Calusa lived on the shores and waterways of the southwest coast of Florida, and controlled most of south Florida. It is believed the population of the tribe reached as many as 50,000. They were not farmers; they mainly survived on fish and shellfish like conchs, crabs, clams, lobsters, and oysters. They fished using nets fashioned from palm tree webbing and used spears to catch eels and turtles. They also hunted small animals using arrowheads made from fish bones. The women and children also contributed to food gathering. The Calusa were first encountered in 1566 when Spanish explorer Pedro Menéndez de Avilés sailed into the area. Within 200 years of this encounter, the Calusa tribe was extinct due to diseases, including smallpox and measles that were brought into the area by the Europeans. It is believed that some members of the Calusa tribe left for Cuba when the Spanish turned Florida over to the British in 1763.

Orange County Courthouse

The Orange County Courthouse in the foreground was built in 1892. The San Juan Hotel in the background was built in 1885. This is in Orlando looking west on Central Avenue (now Central Boulevard) from Main Street (now Magnolia Avenue). The date of the photo is believed to be the late 1890s or early 1900s. The red brick, three-story building, which cost $57,000, was built in the Gothic Revival style with an 80-foot high clock tower. The Orange County Courthouse occupied the building until 1927, when a new courthouse was constructed next door. Afterward, it was used for Orange County offices. On July 30, 1957, the building was condemned and then demolished on December 30, 1957. A new Orange County Courthouse Annex building was constructed on the site. In the late 1990s, the Courthouse Annex was demolished and replaced with an urban park called Heritage Square, owned by Orange County. *Photo courtesy of Matheson History Museum, additional information from* Riches of Central Florida.

People exploring the Old Fort Ruins at New Smyrna, 1904.
Photo courtesy of Library of Congress.

Old Fort Ruins

While the site is called the Old Fort Ruins, there has never been any conclusive evidence to suggest this was actually a fort. Some believe the ruins could be the remains of a mansion or a warehouse but it is generally accepted that the structure was part of an 18th-century settlement established during Florida's British period which lasted from 1763 to 1783. In 1767, the colony of New Smyrna was established by Scottish physician Andrew Turnbull. Along with partner William Duncan, Turnbull received large land grants from the British government in 1766 and he had all the responsibilities of recruiting and hiring people, purchasing slaves, and providing whatever resources that were needed to establish the Smyrna settlement. Turnbull arranged to bring Greek, Minorcan, and Italian settlers to New Smyrna in 1767. He envisioned a colony that would grow cotton and other crops to trade with Great Britain. The ships carrying the settlers were plagued with rough weather and sickness, and 148 of the 1,403 people aboard died before the ships reached Florida. Turnbull and his settlers faced many problems including sickness and drought, causing death and failure of crops. Today, the Old Fort Ruins, which include a series of stone walls with no roof, are located in the heart of what is now called New Smyrna Beach.

A group of cowboys gathered in Pine Barren, northwest of Pensacola, 1904.
Photo courtesy of Martha Morgan, additional information from Florida Department of State.

Pine Barren

Among those pictured here are members of the Morgan family. Their cattle were descended from the European cattle that came over on Spanish ships. Florida's cattle industry dates back to when the early Spanish explorers brought livestock to the Peninsula in the 1500s. From this European stock came the cracker cow, a hardy breed well suited to Florida's hot and swampy climate. The cattle were allowed to roam free and had to be rounded up by cowboys and driven via cattle drives to various ports for sale to Cuba and other Caribbean islands. Florida sold beef to both Confederate and Union troops during the Civil War.

Steven W. Etheridge poses in front of his store, Ethridge Meat Market and Fancy Groceries in Parrish, 1905.
Photo courtesy of Manatee County Public Library System, additional information from ParrishFlorida.com.

Ethridge Meat Market and Fancy Groceries

Steven W. Etheridge's grandfather, Steven H. Ethridge, owned the store with his wife, Mary Ann Freeman Ethridge. They also owned the Ethridge Boarding House, built in 1900. The community dates to the 1870s when Crawford Parrish bought land in the area from William Iredell Turner. The Parrish family raised cattle and sheep. Eventually other families started ranches nearby. A small business district, including a general store, blacksmith's shop, and railroad depot sprang up soon thereafter.

Daytona Beach

The identity of the woman in the photo is not known, but it is likely she was a student of Stetson University in nearby DeLand on a weekend excursion. Other photos in the Stetson University archives show several other women posing for photos in this park and enjoying the beach. In 1905, the road from DeLand to Daytona Beach was nothing more than a sandy trail through the woods. Other outdoor activities enjoyed by Stetson students included boating and visits to the various springs in the area.

A young woman sits under a cabbage palm in a Daytona Beach park, 1905.

Photo courtesy of Stetson University Library Archives.

A typical trapper's home in the Everglades, sparse and desolate, 1907.
Photo courtesy of American Memory/Library of Congress.

The Everglades

At the turn of the 20th century, much of the south Florida coast, including the Everglades, was largely wilderness. Considered uninhabitable, people referred to it as The Big Swamp. Interest in the Everglades centered on exploiting its wildlife, especially the heron and egret for their feathers, and the alligator for its hide. Drastic reductions in wildlife numbers led to legislation protecting plume birds, and the principal focus turned to draining and engineering in the glades for many years.

Worthington Springs

Worthington Springs, a small town about 20 miles north of Gainesville, was once a popular swimming destination. Along the northern bank of the Santa Fe River was a spring-fed concrete pool, a bath house, a dance hall, and a hotel. Visitors flocked to the spring to enjoy its cool sulphur water. At the time, it was believed that bathing in the mineral-rich waters had various health benefits. In the early days, men and women were not permitted to swim together. A straw hat sitting atop a pole beside the pool indicated it was time for the men to swim. A bonnet was draped on the pole when it was the ladies' turn.

Eventually, the spring stopped flowing, the hotel burned down, and the swimming pool crumbled. The only signs of the once thriving facility are a couple of weed-covered foundations. The area is now home to Chastain-Seay Park.

Ladies-only swim time at Worthington Springs in 1909.
Photo courtesy of Tom Moore.

A Seminole family in a dugout canoe, Miami, between 1900 and 1915.

Photo courtesy of Detroit Publishing Co./Library of Congress, additional information from Museum of Florida History.

The Seminole people

The Seminole people have been an important part of Florida history for more than 300 years. Their story of survival and success is remarkable, and their unique culture endures today. The ancestors of today's Seminole people migrated from Alabama and Georgia to Florida in the 1700s and early 1800s. Although they were simply known as Creeks to the British, they spoke different languages and lived in independent towns. Different bands of Creeks established towns in north Florida and traded with both the British and Spanish. After 1765, all Florida Native Americans were referred to as Seminoles. The name may be from the Spanish word cimmarrón meaning "wild" or "untamed." The Seminole people of Florida have persevered despite facing many social, political, and economic pressures. They have proven to be successful at adapting to new circumstances while still preserving important aspects of their culture.

A view from the southwest towards the Cape Florida Light Station, located on the south end of Key Biscayne, around 1900.

Photo courtesy of Department of Commerce, Bureau of Lighthouses, additional information from Florida State Parks.

Cape Florida Light Station

The lighthouse was built in 1825 on Key Biscayne to warn ships of the nearby reef that had spelled doom for many ships over the years. Wrecks were so common in the area that a whole wrecking industry thrived there. Settlers and Seminoles participated. The lighthouse was damaged during the Second Seminole War, and was rebuilt in 1846. It was put out of commission again by a Confederate raiding party in 1861. The light was extinguished in 1878 when it was replaced by the more powerful Fowey Rocks Lighthouse. The rebuilt tower remains and is the oldest standing structure in Miami-Dade County. It was relit in 1978 and is the centerpiece of the 406-acre Bill Baggs Cape Florida Recreation Area.

Thomas Keating's Pier at Daytona Beach, 1900s.
Photo courtesy of Seth Bramson, additional information from City of Daytona Beach.

Thomas Keating's Pier, Daytona Beach

It was built in the late 1890s using palm logs and it extended 600 feet into the ocean. It was located at the end of Main Street where the present pier is located. On January 20, 1920, it was destroyed in a fire. In 1924, Keating sold the remains of the pier to Jeter McMillan who tore it down and began construction of a new pier. The new Pier Casino opened on June 11, 1925, and was 1,000 feet in length. It featured a large Victorian-style ballroom. Top bands of the day performed there. In addition to dances, the Pier Casino was the scene of charity balls, weddings, beauty contests, and social events, as well as civic meetings.

The Railroad Pier, St. Petersburg

The first pier in St. Petersburg was the Orange Belt Railroad Pier, or simply the Railroad Pier. It was built in 1887 and 1888 by Peter Demens, a Russian nobleman turned Florida railroad builder, who previously went by the name Pyotr Alexeyevitch Dementyev. Demens had been convinced by John C. Williams, a wealthy Detroit native who owned land in what would become the town of St. Petersburg, to make the area the western terminus of his Orange Belt Railroad. The line ran from the town of Sanford on the St. Johns river 150 miles to the east. A deal was struck which gave Demens part of Williams's land holdings to complete his railroad. In exchange, Demens was to build a grand hotel and a pier that would extend far enough into the bay to accommodate ships drawing 12 feet of water. The pier extended 3,000 feet into the bay and catered to fishing and shipping industries, while also providing recreational opportunities for residents and tourists. A bathing pavilion with a toboggan ride and fresh water shower was added and it also became very popular with fishermen. As part of the negotiations between the two men, Demens was given naming rights to the fledgling community, and Williams got naming rights to the hotel. Demens named the town St. Petersburg, after his hometown in Russia, and Williams named the hotel The Detroit after his Michigan hometown.

Photo courtesy of Pinellas Memory, additional information from Tampa Bay Times, *St. Pete Pier.*

Annie Mildred McNeill

Annie Mildred McNeill was the winner of The Most Beautiful Baby in Orlando Contest in 1910. She was born in Orlando on July 4, 1909, and lived within a mile of her first home on Lake Eola for all of her 93 years.

Photo courtesy of Lyn Chilton.

Dionisio Valdes around 1910 in his grocery store, La Loma Grocery & Feed.
Photo courtesy of Cynthia Tamargo.

La Loma Grocery & Feed, West Tampa

Dionisio Valdes' grocery story was located on the southwest corner of Armenia Avenue and Cordelia Street in the City of West Tampa (annexed in the 1920s into the City of Tampa). His other adjacent businesses included a cigarette factory called La Floridana and a restaurant, with a boarding house upstairs for the workers in the surrounding cigar factories.

The original building burned down around 1915, but he rebuilt it. Dionisio and Maria Valdes continued to operate the three businesses and the boarding home until Dionisio's untimely death in 1930. He had gone to Port Tampa to visit with a ship's captain from Spain and was run over by a train.

A waterfront view of Captiva Island taken aboard a ferry boat approaching the island, 1910s.
Photo courtesy of Florida Gulf Coast University Library.

Captiva Island

Spanish explorer Juan Ponce de León is said to have been the first European to visit Sanibel Island in 1513, but due to attacks from the resident Calusa, permanent settlement was not possible. Eventually, diseases wiped out the Calusa people. Legend has it Captiva Island was a hideout for pirates in the 1800s. One of those pirates, Jose Gaspar, allegedly held his female prisoners captive there, hence the name Captiva. However, the legend is more fiction than fact; the only clue to the origin of the name can be traced back to a real estate pamphlet. Before the Sanibel Causeway was completed in 1963 and opened for traffic from the mainland, residents, visitors, and supplies were ferried by boat.

Robert Hungerford Normal and Industrial School

Robert Hungerford Normal and Industrial School was a segregated high school for African Americans in Eatonville. The school was founded by Professor and Mrs. Russell C. Calhoun in 1897. Both the professor and his wife attended the Tuskegee Institute, of which he was a graduate. Mr. E. C. Hungerford donated 160 acres of land to the school in memory of his late son, Robert, who died due to yellow fever. Robert was a doctor and had cared for a sick African American boy whom no one else would help, even after Robert himself became ill.

The groundwork for the school was made possible thanks to donors not only from Florida, but throughout the country. The first cash donation for Hungerford was given by Miss Mary Brown of Winter Park, and the second was $400 through Booker T. Washington of Tuskegee.

Later on, Mr. George B. Cluett, the head manufacturer of Troy, New York, donated $8,000 towards the construction of a second building, and an additional $4,000 towards the purchase of an orange grove near campus. Although Cluett Hall was burned in 1922, it was replaced by a stone structure bearing the same name only a

TOP: J.H. Alfred Cluett Hall, Hungerford Normal and Industrial School, Eatonville, 1910.

RIGHT: Principal's Home, Robert Hungerford Normal and Industrial School, Eatonville, 1910.

Photos courtesy of Matheson History Museum.

year and a half later. Cluett also contributed a major sum towards the dining hall, which he himself insisted be named Calhoun Hall. Additionally, he gave $500 annually towards expenses for a number of years.

Hungerford was a private school, offering Grades 6 through 12 with dorms for both girls and boys. The institution was equipped with a dining hall, chapel, library, manual training shops, laundry, home economics laboratory, barn, farmland, and facilities for teaching business subjects.

It embraced both college preparatory and vocational, including subjects such as English, Latin, history, general science, biology, algebra, geometry, manual training (industrial arts), and home economics. The school also taught typing, bookkeeping, agriculture, and physical education.

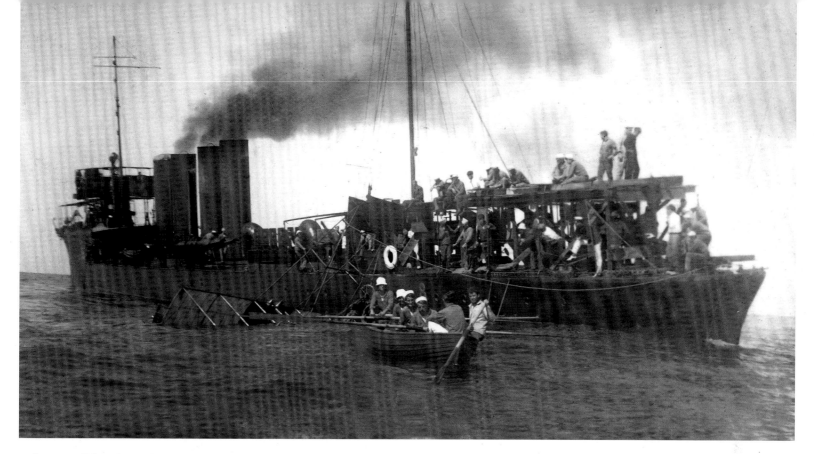

First flight from Florida to Cuba

Aviator and later politician John Alexander Douglas McCurdy's plane in the water alongside the Navy destroyer USS *Paulding*, January 30, 1911, the day McCurdy flew to Havana, Cuba, from Key West, Florida. He arranged for there to be six American torpedo boat destroyers evenly spaced between Florida and Cuba, each puffing out smoke as a means of navigation and potential rescue. A burned bearing on the crankshaft forced McCurdy to glide to a gentle landing on the ocean within sight of Havana. McCurdy had fitted his biplane with two pontoons — another first — in the event he was forced to ditch. Cuban President José Miguel Gómez held a state banquet where it was announced that McCurdy would be awarded $18,000 in prize money, but when McCurdy opened the envelope he found nothing but newspaper clippings. The flight produced three world records. At 90 miles, it was the longest flight over water, the longest time spent aloft (two hours, 20 minutes), and he was the first to fly out of sight of land on a clear day. Though mechanical problems forced him to ditch his plane less than a mile short of his destination, McCurdy's flight is widely considered to be the first flight from Key West to Cuba.

Photo by Albert McCarthy, courtesy of Keys Library, additional information from FIU and U.S. Navy Archives.

Frank P. Goodman is on his horse Old Dan in front of the Frank C. Gardner home in Lake Alfred, sometime after 1911, which is when Gardner arrived from Fargo, North Dakota. *Photo courtesy of Lake Alfred Historical Society, additional information from City of Lake Alfred.*

Lake Alfred

Lake Alfred was first settled as a military outpost, Fort Cummings, in 1839. The Fort closed down in the mid-1840s and the area once again became a remote region. In 1887 the South Florida Railroad came through, connecting Sanford and Tampa, as part of the rail system constructed by William Van Fleet. A lumber mill and turpentine still were constructed and named the Lake Alfred Lumber Company. Around 1907, the J.C. Cox family came to Lake Alfred and acquired two 40-acre citrus groves. This was the beginning of the citrus age and the beginning of the growth of the city. In 1910, Frank C. Gardner of Fargo, North Dakota, and his partners, Edward Pierce, James Banks, and W.F. Froemke formed the Florida Fruitlands Company and purchased considerable acreage, cleared the pine stumps and planted citrus. The city was incorporated in 1913 as Fargo, but was renamed in 1915 after its namesake water body, Lake Alfred. In 1912, Fruitlands President Frank C. Gardner built the first Presbyterian Church. The Lake Alfred Women's Club was formally created in 1917. In the early 1920s, the Fruitlands Company built a hotel under the direction of Frank P. Goodman, and investors came to Lake Alfred by train or car to purchase land, spurring a development boom. Lake Alfred grew rapidly as stores were built and citrus processing and packing plants began to sprout up. Citrus was the main industry and remained so for many decades afterwards.

McNeill family of Orlando

(L to R) Edward Herndon McNeill, Sr. (1859-1923) and Captain William Henry Swinton, holding the reins of his horse named Eola. (The name of the horse's sibling on the left is unknown.) Mr. McNeill was an entrepreneur who moved around the state at the turn of the 20th century. He owned several turpentine stills in Lake, Marion, and Orange Counties; bought and sold land; and did some farming. He eventually settled in Orlando and raised a family of five children.

This picture was taken circa 1912, standing next to his cornfield by his home at 309 E Robinson Street. Lake Eola Park, which can be seen in the background, was a popular gathering spot for residents; concerts were held in the bandshell.

Annie Mildred McNeill is standing in her front yard, which also happened to be the banks of Lake Eola in Orlando in 1912. She is proudly displaying her Kewpie doll, a cupid-inspired doll which was very popular with young girls. In the distance, you can just make out the Confederate monument adorned with an unnamed Confederate soldier dubbed by locals as Johnny Reb. The daughter of Edward Herndon McNeill, Sr., McNeill would go on to become an influential force in both the business and social worlds of Orlando. She was active in the First Presbyterian Church downtown and sang in the choir. She was proud of her career as a secretary and was the President of the local chapter of The National Secretaries Association in the 1950s. Her high-profile positions included secretary to Rollins College President Jack B Critchfield in the 1970s. Her career continued into the 1980s, working for Tax Collector Earl K. Wood.

Photos courtesy of Lyn Chilton.

Florida East Coast Railway Key West Extension

Henry Flagler and his wife, Mary Lily, arrive aboard the first train to Key West for the celebration marking the completion of the Florida East Coast Railway Key West Extension, January 22, 1912. The talk of a canal being built across the Isthmus of Panama had long intrigued Flagler. For this reason, he kept the option of expanding his railway from Miami to Key West a possibility. He realized that Key West, the United States' closest deep-water port to the Canal, would not only take advantage of Cuban and Latin American trade, but would also allow significant trade possibilities with California. When the United States announced its intention to build the Canal in 1905, Flagler knew it was time to expand his railroad to Key West. The construction of the Over-Sea Railroad linking the Florida Keys to the mainland was the culmination of eight years of work and the last major project undertaken by Flagler. With the estimated cost of $50 million, it was referred to as Flagler's Folly by friends and the media alike. On May 20th, 1913, a little more than a year after he arrived in Key West on his train, Henry Flagler passed away at the age of 83 in his home in Palm Beach.

Photo courtesy of Digital Library of America, additional information from The Smithsonian and Miami History.

Moon Lake

Pearle Swartsel McCreary and Ola Douglas taking a boat ride on Moon Lake in New Port Richey in the summer of 1913. Pearle was born in 1886 in Emporia, Kansas. Her family moved to Tarpon Springs from Kansas City, Kansas, when she was 12 years old. In 1929, Edward A. Haley purchased 8,000 acres of land adjacent to Moon Lake and established the Moon Lake Gardens and Dude ranch. When it officially opened to the public on August 4, 1933, it was considered a sportsman's paradise and included exotic gardens, bridle paths, a rodeo ring, a hunting preserve stocked with deer, wild turkeys, pheasants, quail, and various other types of game. Bears, alligators, and wildcats already inhabited the area. Moon Lake was stocked with largemouth bass from the hatchery on the property. The massive lodge included a clubhouse, complete with an auditorium, a casino, a dining room, a 60-foot bar, a dance floor, and a porch surrounding the entire structure. Many famous guests were known to have frequented the establishment. The onset of World War II brought declining business and it was forced to close in 1942.

Photo courtesy of Jody McCreary/Manatee County Public Library System.

Pensacola Naval Aeronautical Station

On February 2, 1914, Lieutenant J. H. Towers and Ensign G. Chevalier made the first flight from the Pensacola Naval Aeronautical Station (or Naval Air Station, or simply N.A.S.). The 20-minute flight covered the military reservation and Bayou Grande. Towers founded Pensacola N.A.S. in January 1914, when he brought seven aircraft, 42 men, and portable hangars from Annapolis to use for training other aviators.

Photo courtesy of New York Public Library, additional information from the Clewiston Museum.

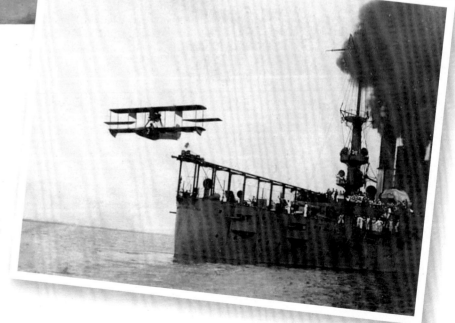

November 5, 1915, the first catapult launch of an aircraft from the USS *North Carolina* anchored off the Naval Aeronautical Station at Pensacola was made by Henry C. Mustin. He helped establish the Naval Air Station on the site of the old Navy Yard at Warrington in 1914. Mustin Beach and the Mustin Beach Officers Club at NAS Pensacola are named for him.

Photo courtesy of PICRYL, additional information from Pensapedia, and Naval History and Heritage Command.

Socrum

Postmaster John Witter (on top step, 1858-1953), in front of his store/post office in Socrum, a community about 10 miles northwest of Lakeland, 1915. The store/post office was established in 1907 and operated until 1918. It was located on the south side of West Socrum Loop Road, just west of Old Dade City Road, near present day Socrum Elementary School. According to tradition, the name is a variation of "soak 'em", due to it being a marshy area. An alternate derivation is a conjunction of soak and rum, as early settlers would keep barrels of rum both relatively cool and safe from native populations by immersing the barrels in a nearby lake which is still known as Indian Lake.

Photo courtesy of Ruth Anne Witter Maloy, additional information from Wikipedia.

The steamship *The City of Sarasota* at Cortez around 1915.
Photo courtesy of Manatee County in Photos.

The City of Sarasota

This was not the ship's original name. Beginning in October 1895, the *Mistletoe* began a regular schedule, bringing passengers and goods every Monday, Wednesday, and Friday and returning to Tampa on Tuesdays, Thursdays, and Saturdays. In October of 1910, while being overhauled in Tampa, the *Mistletoe* sank during a hurricane. After being raised, the steamship was enlarged and outfitted to carry 200 passengers as well as cargo. In its new form, it was christened *The City of Sarasota* on February 6, 1911. By 1917, *The City of Sarasota* ended its runs to Sarasota. It was converted into a barge, but it did not function as well as hoped and was pulled onto shore and burned.

Spanish Flu pandemic, Miami

The influenza pandemic of 1918 came to a head in the city of Miami as well as the surrounding areas. Miami was optimistic at the time; the city was less than 25 years old. Business interests teamed up for a full advertisement touting Miami by saying "The Golden Gate of Opportunity has been flung wide open to all who will deserve success," but things were about to change. Between March and July of 1918, the pandemic killed thousands worldwide, spread by contact between people. Because we were at war and morale was a concern, the government did its best to censor news about the pandemic. Like the rest of the United States at the time, Miami did not take the pandemic seriously until it reached the city. On October 9th, just a week before the deadliest day, the headline in the *Miami Herald* read: "There is no reason to get excited over the situation, which is not even grave. The disease will rapidly disappear if the people will use ordinary precautions and take care of themselves." A week later, the *Miami Herald* finally acknowledged the presence of the pandemic and provided information and advice on how to avoid getting infected. The City Board of Health stepped in and ordered the closing of all stores and restaurants except for necessary businesses such as drug stores. On November 1st, the city began to reopen slowly. The *Miami Herald* wrote "The Dark Month of October is behind us." The Miami Board of Health declared that the pandemic was over. Over 1,200 Floridians lost their lives in the month of October as a result of the pandemic.

A sailor and wife during the Spanish Flu Pandemic in Miami, October 1918.
Photo courtesy of Miami Dade Public Library System, additional information from Miami Herald *Archives,* New Times, History Miami.

Dade City

The Martin family on the porch of their home in Dade City in 1918. If you look closely, you can see the star hanging in the window featuring the words "Over There" for the eldest son, C.W. Martin, who was with the infantry in France when this photo was taken during WWI. He was wounded in the Meuse-Argonne Offensive, which was a part of the final Allied offensive of World War I, and was the largest and deadliest operation of the American Expeditionary Forces (AEF) in that war. Over a million American soldiers participated and over 26,000 soldiers were killed in action.

Photo courtesy of Larry Martin.

INSET: One of the patriotic flyers seen in the window of the Martin home.

Intersection of Broadway and Monument Avenue in Kissimmee, looking southwest 1919.

Photo courtesy of Matheson History Museum, additional information from Osceola County and RICHES of Central Florida.

Kissimmee

The name Kissimmee can be traced back to the language of the Jororo people. The Jororo were Native Americans that inhabited the Kissimmee Valley region of Central Florida before European settlers arrived. It was here that the Creeks and other Native peoples of the South-Central United States fled in the mid to late 18th century. The Seminole, a conglomeration of Native American peoples and escaped slaves, settled in the Kissimmee River Valley and in the swamplands of Central and South Florida because of their tactically defendable positions. The original Euro-American name of Kissimmee was Allendale, named so in honor of Confederate Major J. H. Allen, the operator of the *Mary Belle*, the first cargo steamboat along the Kissimmee River. The town served as a small trading post on the banks of Lake Tohopekaliga. Following the Civil War, Hamilton Disston, the owner of Disston Saw Company of Philadelphia, Pennsylvania, purchased four million acres of land in the area at a total cost of $1 million. In 1881, he began to drain the area and deepen the Kissimmee River, thus allowing goods to be shipped into the Gulf of Mexico. When the city was incorporated in 1883, it was renamed Kissimmee. During the 1920s, Kissimmee, as well as much of Florida, experienced a land boom. The citrus industry and the cattle industry flourished during the following decades. Kissimmee experienced later periods of growth in the 1950s and the 1970s, as a result of the opening of Walt Disney World.

Ormond Beach

Looking northeast towards Granada Boulevard, Ormond Beach, 1910s. Seen here are homes along the beach, the Hotel Ormond trolley, and the Ormond Beach Golf Club. The horse-drawn trolley transported guests eastward from the hotel to the golf course and beach. The Hotel Ormond was built in 1887 by John Anderson and Joseph Price. It was later purchased and enlarged by Henry Flagler in the 1890s.

Photo courtesy of New York Public Library.

Tampa

Nicely dressed children from the Valdes family pose on the steps leading up to the Lafayette Street bridge from Plant Park in Tampa, Easter 1920. From left to right are Palmira, Francisco, Angel, and Dulce Maria. On November 18, 1963, President John F. Kennedy visited Tampa. His motorcade traveled across this bridge. Four days later, on November 22, 1963, his assassination in Dallas would shock the world. The road was renamed in his honor in 1964 by unanimous vote of the Tampa City Council. The bridge is now known as the John F. Kennedy Boulevard Bridge.

Photo courtesy of Cynthia Tamargo.

Central Avenue, St. Petersburg

A view from the 1920s looking down Central Avenue from around 5th Street toward what is now the new pier in downtown St. Petersburg. The pier seen to the right of Central is at the end of 1st Avenue South and was known as the Railroad Pier. It was built by Peter Demens of Orange Belt Railroad fame and later purchased by Henry Plant. That area is now known as Demens Landing.

Photo courtesy of Vale Tim Fillmon.

Orange groves of Lake Alfred

Ten-year-old orange groves in Lake Alfred, 1920. The dwelling in the middle of the photo is the Frank P. Goodman house on Carolina Avenue. The cluster of buildings on the left is Seminole Avenue and Main Street. Frank P. Goodman was a prominent figure in civic affairs of the Lake Alfred and Winter Haven area. He came to the community in 1913 from Fargo, North Dakota.

Photo courtesy of Lake Alfred Historical Society.

The *City of Melrose*

A group of men on board the *City of Melrose* at the Melrose Landing, 1920. Docked alongside a railroad bridge next to a waiting Seaboard railway car, they are either loading or unloading their supplies. Before automobiles and highways, goods were shipped by boat and train for distribution. A route of the Seaboard Air Line Railroad Company ran through Alachua County on the way to Tampa.

Photo courtesy of Matheson History Museum.

Chief Cory Osceola

Cory Osceola (on the right), and his extended family standing in front of a chickee (the Seminole word for house) at a Seminole tourist camp near the Tamiami Trail, 1920s. This photo was used to produce postcards sold to tourists. These camps became a way for the Seminole to earn revenue from visitors who were eager to learn how they lived. Born in 1893, Cory was a great-grandson of the Seminole War hero Osceola, who died in 1838. In 1922, Cory's left arm was amputated at the shoulder after a train accident in Fort Lauderdale. Although the term "chief" isn't often used in Seminole culture, Cory Osceola was an important leader and used the title when identifying himself in the white world. He frequently met and corresponded with presidents and governors concerning land negotiations and other legal battles. Newspaper reports from the time chronicle his long history of activism on behalf of the tribe. In 1931, he halted President Herbert Hoover's attempt to appoint a Seminole from Oklahoma as chief of the Florida Seminoles for a day in an effort to sign away tribal land. Cory passed away in 1978.

Photo courtesy of Stetson University Library Archives, additional information from the Orange County Library.

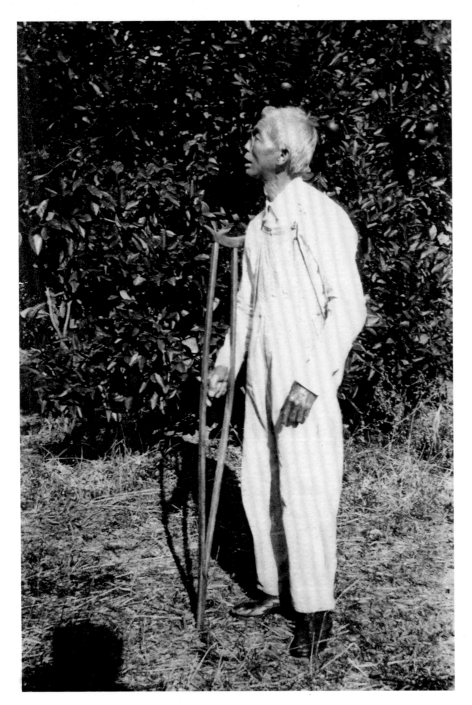

Lue Gim Gong

Lue Gim Gong looks over his orange grove in DeLand, 1922. Lue (August 24, 1857 – June 3, 1925), a Chinese American immigrant in the late nineteenth century, was an accomplished horticulturalist who contributed to the growth of the American citrus industry by developing a cold-resistant orange tree and other plants. He is considered a citrus pioneer, known for cross-pollination techniques and hybrid fruits. In 2000, he was recognized as a Great Floridian by the Florida Department of State for his significant contributions.

Photo courtesy of Stetson University Library Archives.

A New River scene, Fort Lauderdale, 1922.

Photo courtesy of Jacksonville Library Collection, additional information from History Fort Lauderdale *and* The Sun-Sentinel.

New River

According to Native American legend, the New River appeared overnight after a storm or earthquake which collapsed the roof of an underground waterway. The Seminole awoke the next morning to find a river where there had been land. They called it Himmarshee, or "new water." Despite its name, it is not a river, but a tidal estuary composed of many tributary canals. It is connected to the Everglades through man-made canals, passes through Fort Lauderdale, and connects to the intercoastal Waterway and the Atlantic Ocean at Port Everglades cut. The direct route to the Atlantic Ocean made the New River a convenient area to operate for rum runners during prohibition in the 1920s. Bootleggers could sail directly from the Bahamas up the New River to distribute their cargo. Law enforcement began cracking down by conducting "rum raids" which slowed the activity. This earned Fort Lauderdale the nickname "Fort Liquordale."

Palafox Street Wharf, Pensacola, 1922.
Photo courtesy of Gulf Coast Maritime Digital Portal Project, UWF Library and the Miami Herald *Archives.*

Palafox Street Wharf, Pensacola

In the 1920s, excursion boats operated from Palafox Street Wharf offering excursions to Navy Yard, coastal forts, Pensacola Lighthouse, and the Coast Guard lifesaving station on Santa Rosa Island. Captain Bennie Edmundson purchased a large steamship, *The Baldwin*, capable of transporting 400 passengers to Santa Rosa Island.

At the end of WW1, Captain Edmundson made a deal to reopen the island to development and excursions in March 1919. In 1931, the maritime excursion business of Palafox Street Wharf peaked with the completion of the Pensacola Bay and Santa Rosa Sound bridges that enabled land and vehicle access to the resorts and beaches on the island.

Roman Pools, Miami Beach

Beachside bathing casinos were a popular gathering place for sunbathers in the early 20th century. Despite the name, they had nothing to do with gambling; they were actually bathing pavilions, a place where you could go to enjoy the beach, or swim in the pool. At one time, there were five bathing casinos in Miami Beach. The most famous was the Everglades Cabana Club, later named the Roman Pools. Built in 1920 by John Collins and Russell Pancoast, the casino was located on the block between 22nd and 23rd streets and Collins Avenue, just south of the Roney Plaza. Originally, it started as the Miami Beach Casino, but within a short time it was renamed to Fisher's St. Johns Casino with Carl Fisher as proprietor.

By 1926, the name was changed again to Roman Pools. Sometime in the late 1940s, it was renamed Everglades Cabana Club. It featured a Dutch-inspired windmill which supplied fresh saltwater into two large swimming pools. Swimming and diving events were held and they drew large crowds. It grew to become a major entertainment venue complete with nightclubs, restaurants, show rooms, dancing, and various stores. The casino survived several hurricanes, and stayed in business until the early 1950s. The windmill remained standing until the building's demolition in the early 1960s, following a fire.

Roman Pools Bathing Casino, Miami Beach, 1925
Photo courtesy of Miami Dade Public Library, additional information from Seth Bramson and Miami Design Preservation League.

Liquor raid at the Dugout Restaurant, Miami, 1925

Prohibition was officially implemented on January 1, 1920, but Miami had already enacted a county-wide prohibition six years earlier. It was believed the 18th Amendment would end the scourge of alcohol consumption. Instead, the law was loosely enforced and gave rise to an underground syndicate of organizations that would fill America's thirst for alcohol. While local and federal regulations banned the sale and consumption, most of Miami largely ignored the law. Proprietors of legitimate businesses also set up hidden rooms, known as speakeasies, to meet the demand for liquor.

Photo courtesy of Miami Dade Public Library System, additional information from Miami New Times.

Granada Entrance, Coral Gables, 1925

Constructed in 1922 and designed by city designer Denman Fink and landscape architect Frank Button, this was the first of seven entrances planned for the city of Coral Gables. Reported to be inspired by similar entrance gates in Spain, the 340-foot-long structure features a 40-foot arch that spans Granada Boulevard, with a pergola to both sides that includes wing walls with sitting ledges. The oolitic limestone was hand-cut into blocks to use in the creation of the arched structure, which allows vehicles to pass underneath it while entering and leaving the city.

Photo courtesy of Coral Gables Memory/FIU Library/Fishbaugh Collection.

Bayou Chico Yacht Club

Storm damage at Bayou Chico Yacht Club in Pensacola in September 1926 after the Great Miami Hurricane devastated the area. The storm was a large and intense tropical cyclone that devastated the Greater Miami area and the U.S. Gulf Coast as well as causing extensive damage in the Bahamas. Wind records at Pensacola indicate that the city encountered sustained winds of hurricane force for more than 20 hours, including winds above 100 mph for five hours. The storm tide destroyed nearly all waterfront structures on Pensacola Bay in 1926.

Photo courtesy of Cottrell Collection/University of West Florida.

Swimming competition at the Miami Biltmore Hotel in Coral Gables, 1927.
Photo courtesy of Miami Dade Public Library System.

Miami Biltmore Hotel, Coral Gables

In 1925, land developer George E. Merrick joined forces with Bowman-Biltmore Hotels president John McEntee Bowman at the height of the Florida land boom to build "a great hotel ... which would not only serve as a hostelry to the crowds which were thronging to Coral Gables but also would serve as a center of sports and fashion." Visitors included the Duke and Duchess of Windsor, Ginger Rogers, Judy Garland, Bing Crosby, Al Capone, and assorted Roosevelts and Vanderbilts as frequent guests. Shortly after the hotel opened, the Great Miami Hurricane of 1926 hit. The hotel was undamaged, but the disaster was the beginning of the end of the land boom. The hotel was sold in September 1931 to millionaire Henry Latham Doherty. A large part of the hotel's revenue in the 1930s came from aquatic galas. Large crowds would come out on a Sunday afternoon to watch the synchronized swimmers, bathing beauties, and alligator wrestling. Johnny Weissmuller, before he was known as Tarzan, broke a world record at the pool. During World War II, it was converted to a hospital and renamed Pratt General Hospital. After the war, it reverted back to being the Biltmore Hotel.

Pompano Race Track, Labor Day Races, September, 1927. *Photo courtesy of Miami Dade Public Library, additional information from Florida Online Journals, Isle Pompano Park, and Daily Racing Form.*

Pompano Race Track

The Pompano Race Track was announced on June 6, 1925, in local news reports. The headline read "Broward County will have a race track and plant fully in keeping with Miami Jockey Club." The goal was to establish another horse track halfway between Palm Beach and Miami. In July 1925, Governor John W. Martin approved the race track to be located one half-mile south of Pompano and one half-mile west of the Dixie Highway. The Pompano Race Track was scheduled to open Christmas Day 1926 with the running of a $3,000 Christmas Handicap. A large crowd of spectators was expected from Dade, Broward, and Palm Beach. The grand opening was a success; it was witnessed by a crowd of 15,000 to 20,000 people. Pompano Race Track became Pompano Harness Track in 1964. It is now a casino.

Ponce de Leon Plaza, Coral Gables, 1927

The plaza is named for the Spanish explorer, Juan Ponce de León who led the first expedition to Florida in 1513. The plaza was designed in 1925 by the city's landscape architect, Frank Button, and Denman Fink, the city's artistic director. Fink was the uncle of city founder and builder George Merrick who credited Fink for heavily influencing him in his creation of Coral Gables. Fink was an acclaimed artist whose artistic input can be felt in the city's early entrances, plazas, and spring-fed Venetian Pool.

Photo courtesy of Coral Gables Memory/FIU Library, additional information from the Coral Gables Museum,

Loop Drive, Ormond, 1929. *Photo courtesy of Rinhart Collection/University of Miami Library.*

Ormond's Scenic Loop & Trail

In the early years of the 20th century, as more people began to own automobiles, day touring became a fashionable pastime. For decades, Ormond's Scenic Loop & Trail has been a popular, picturesque drive, with approximately 30 miles of roadways lined with luxurious palms and shaded by majestic and stately oaks. The drive winds along the Atlantic Ocean and back along the Halifax River.

Fort Lauderdale boatbuilders

These carpenters are on a break at a boatyard in Fort Lauderdale, 1920s. Pioneer Edwin King was a master carpenter and boatbuilder. He came to the area in 1895 and was responsible for building the first school, as well as several of the area residences, including his own. In the 1910s, he opened a boatyard, which stood on the south side of the New River just west of the Andrews Avenue Bridge. Though unconfirmed, this boat construction crew taking a break in the 1920s may have been working for him.

There was great demand for boats in the area. As early as 1922, Fort Lauderdale was called the Venice of America with its claim to fame of 165 miles of navigable waterways in and about the city. Boating and water sports were a major draw for tourists and new residents, and its many marinas enhanced the city's reputation as a recreational boating epicenter for people from around the world.

Photo courtesy of Angela Mosely.

Trolley, Jacksonville

Beginning in the late 1800s, trolleys (or streetcars) moved people around the city of Jacksonville. At first they were pulled along tracks by horses. Eventually, electricity provided the source of power via an outstretched arm on top of the streetcar connected to overhead electrical wires. The trolleys stopped running in 1936, replaced with buses which were cheaper to operate. In this 1920s photo, two men are driving the #144 trolley along Main Street. Perhaps they are taking their fares to the Orpheum Theatre for the show put on by Interstate Vaudeville, a vaudeville booking and exhibition company. The South was slow to accept vaudeville as a legitimate form of entertainment; such theater was often characterized as a Gateway to Hell in the popular media of the time. *Photo courtesy of Gary Kirkland.*

Orlando

Orlando, The City Beautiful, as seen from the east side of Lake Eola looking west, late 1920s. The slogan dates back to at least 1908 when local officials borrowed it from the City Beautiful urban planning movement transforming places like Cleveland, Detroit, and Denver. In those communities, progressive city planners designed parks, museums, and public plazas to beautify and organize the urban landscape. In Orlando, a rural cow town at the time, City Beautiful represented something different, an aspiration rather than a reality. A hope that the small assortment of ranchers and citrus growers could one day develop into a full-fledged city. It did, and the nickname stuck. Today, it's included on Orlando's city seal. You can read it on signs and markers throughout the city.

Photo courtesy of the Florida Hospital Heritage Collection, additional information from Neil J. Young.

Aloma Country Club, Winter Park

The clubhouse opened with a big New Year's Eve party, December 31, 1926, to welcome the new year. Dr. Roland F. Hotard, with a group of investors, formed the Winter Park Golf Estates, Inc., and purchased 360 acres of land where AdventHealth Winter Park (formerly Winter Park Memorial Hospital) is located today, to build a golf course and golf community. The anticipated growth never really materialized beyond a few short years. The Florida land boom of the late 1920s collapsed, and the Great Depression sadly relegated the distinctive clubhouse to slow decay. In the early 1950s, the site became the choice location to build the Winter Park Memorial Hospital.

Aloma Country Club in Winter Park, late 1920s.
Photo courtesy of the Florida Hospital Heritage Collection, additional information from Patsy Ann Carter Taylor.

Fort Myers Beach arches

The coquina rock arches date to 1924 during the Florida land boom. They were created by home developer Tom Phillips to highlight the dramatic transition in crossing to Fort Myers Beach. The arches allowed traffic to flow both on and off the island under a separate arch, with sidewalk arches on each side, allowing for safe pedestrian traffic as well. They remained for 55 years to the delight of many but were razed in 1979 to make way for the Matanzas Pass Bridge from San Carlos Island to the barrier island of Fort Myers Beach. There has been an ongoing effort to restore the arches. It has taken several years of proposals, negotiation, and more than a few dead ends, but a single arch replica is expected to be built on a county park in the town of Fort Myers Beach.

Lillian McLean and Olin Gay in front of the Fort Myers Beach arches, mid to late 1920s.
Photos courtesy of David Renz.

Lake Fairview spouting well, Orlando

The Lake Fairview spouting well first appeared in the early years of the 20th century at the Davis-McNeill farm on the lake's south side, where a geyser began to erupt about every six minutes and reached heights of 75 to 100 feet. According to a short article in *Scientific American* magazine in 1911, Orlando officials had faced problems because the city's lakes often overflowed — an especially irksome problem for truck farmers near Lake Fairview, who found their fields flooded. The remedy was to drive pipes hundreds of feet into the ground in search of underground passageways into which the excess water could be drained. At Lake Fairview, the top of one such pipe near the lake's edge sat only five inches below the water's surface. The article suggested the jets of water rushed up out of the pipe when air pressure built up in a natural underground chamber and reached a critical point. Soon farm manager R.D. Eunice asked spectators for a small admission fee; those who didn't want to pay just stationed themselves across the lake to watch from a distance, waiting through the interval between spouts. The pipe was capped in the 1930s, and Orlando's spouting well was no more.

Photo courtesy of the Florida Hospital Heritage Collection, additional information from the Orange County Regional History Center.

Fort Marion, St. Augustine

Originally constructed by the Spanish in the late 17th century, the stone Castillo de San Marcos replaced a previous wooden fortification. The need for a stone fort became apparent after the English buccaneer Robert Searle burnt most of the settlement in 1668. The new stone fort was constructed between 1672 and 1695. Over the course of its history, the Castillo de San Marcos has been controlled by Spain, Britain, the Confederate States, and the United States. The fort was never taken in battle, despite being besieged on two occasions. It has served at various times as a prison, including during the Second Seminole War when the famous Seminole leader Osceola was a prisoner there. The Castillo de San Marcos was declared a National Monument in 1900. In 1942, it was renamed Castillo de San Marcos, reverting to its original Spanish name.

Sophia Warken Lantz visiting Fort Marion in St. Augustine, 1930.
Photo courtesy of Donna Starratt.

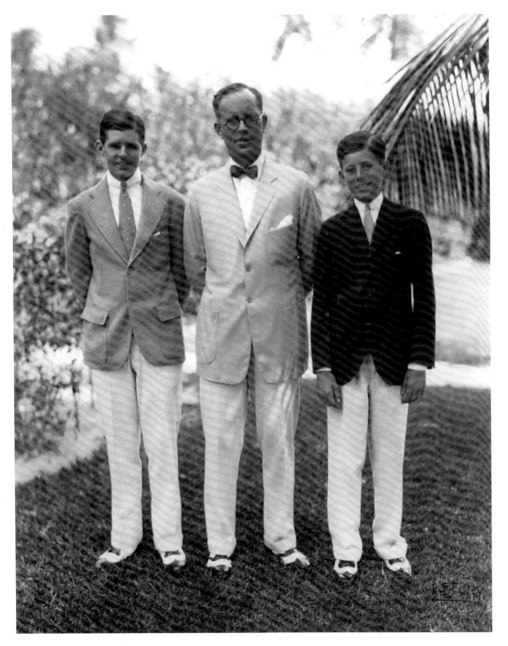

The Kennedys in Palm Beach

Joseph P. Kennedy, Sr. with sons Joseph P. Kennedy, Jr. (left) and John F. Kennedy (right), Palm Beach, Florida, 1931. The Kennedys began vacationing in Palm Beach as early as the 1910s. In 1933, Joseph P. Kennedy, Sr. purchased La Querida for $120,000, a Mediterranean-style estate designed 10 years prior by architect Addison Mizner. The home at 1095 N. Ocean Boulevard recently sold for $70 million. During John F. Kennedy's presidency, the compound became known as the Winter White House.

Photo by E. F. Foley, courtesy of Library of Congress.

Members of the Seminole Tribe, Miami

Members of the Seminole Tribe are meeting with a voting instructor to learn how to cast their ballots in Miami, 1931. In 1924, Representative Homer Snyder of New York proposed the bill which was known as *The Indian Citizenship Act* which granted citizenship to the Indigenous peoples of the United States. The challenge was that the 14th Amendment clearly states that a citizen is anyone who is born in the United States. However, the courts ruled at the time that it did not apply to Indigenous people. It was signed into law by President Calvin Coolidge on June 2, 1924. One of the arguments in the bill's favor was the fact that Native Americans served in the Armed Forces during World War I.

Photo courtesy of Miami Dade Public Library System, additional information from Library of Congress, Britannica, and National Institute of Health.

Penn Cash Grocery Store, Bradenton

The Penn Cash Grocery Store opened to the public in early 1916. At the time, it was considered a supermarket, selling everything from washboards to meats and fresh produce. By the 1930s, the store became known for stocking health foods, which was a cutting-edge idea for the time. The owners picked the location on the corner of Eighth Avenue and Thirteenth Street West because it allowed for goods to be delivered to area homes by motorcycle, another early innovation by the owners Harry E. Mower and Leslie Chapman.

Penn Cash grocery with delivery motorcycle, 802 13th Street West, Bradenton, 1934.
Photo courtesy of Manatee County Public Library System, additional information from Manatee County Historical Society.

Men and mules working on the Cross Florida Barge Canal at Ocala, October 11, 1935.

Photo courtesy of New York Public Library.

Cross Florida Barge Canal

For centuries, explorers, pioneers, businessmen, politicians, and, no doubt, the area's Indigenous peoples have dreamed of a waterway linking the Atlantic Ocean and the Gulf of Mexico. Construction was first proposed in the 16th century by the Spanish, and in 1818, Secretary of War John C. Calhoun again proposed the idea. Not only were they seeking a shortcut, but they were also looking to solve the problem of shipwrecks caused by strong currents, shallow water, storms, and piracy. The notion of constructing such a passageway proved to be too much of a financial and logistical undertaking. In the 1930s, the project was revisited and promoted as a way to help stimulate the economy and provide jobs during the Great Depression. President Franklin D. Roosevelt approved five million dollars for the project and on September 19, 1935, work began. A year later in 1936, Michigan Senator Arthur H. Vandenberg challenged the project stating it never received approval from Congress. Additionally, poor labor practices and environmental concerns were being raised, such as potential damage to the Florida aquifer, thus jeopardizing drinking water. Funding was also running out and work on the project came to a stop. In 1942, Congress passed a bill authorizing a revised canal plan as a national defense project but never appropriated the money as more pressing war needs took priority. Years passed, and in 1963, the plan was once again given consent. President Lyndon B. Johnson traveled to Pataka in 1964 for a ceremonial groundbreaking, kicking off the project once more. Environmental activists regrouped and challenged the initiative, and finally in 1971 President Richard Nixon signed an executive order halting the plan. Though this may be seen as an environmental win, parts of the project were completed, including locks, dams, bridges, and canals that to this day adversely impact the natural water flows. Thankfully, the entire project was never realized.

Bok Tower and Gardens, Lake Wales

Bok Tower and Gardens, founded by Edward William Bok, opened to the public in 1929. Edward was born October 9, 1863, in Den Helder, Netherlands, and when he was six years old immigrated to the United States with his parents and a brother. The family settled in Brooklyn, New York, where they lived in poverty. He came to the United States without knowing the language, yet only 20 years later, at the age of 26, he became editor of the *Ladies' Home Journal*, a position he held from 1889 to 1919. During his tenure, he was successful in helping to bring awareness and change to many areas, including wildlife conservation, pure food, sanitation, and women's suffrage. In 1921, he won the Pulitzer Prize for his autobiography *The Americanization of Edward Bok* (1920). At the age of 56, after 30 highly successful and interesting years in publishing, he escaped the cold of Pennsylvania and moved to Lake Wales where he created a sanctuary and gardens. The centerpiece of the gardens is the 205-foot-tall Gothic and art deco Singing Tower. Made of coquina rock, marble, brick, and steel, the tower houses a 60-bell carillon which is still played regularly. Bok passed away within sight of the tower on January 9, 1930, and is buried near the base of it in front of the great brass door.

Janice Barbara Gay and friend at Bok Tower Gardens in Lake Wales, 1935.
Photo courtesy of David Renz; young Janice Gay is his mother.

Coconut Grove

America's entry into World War I in 1917 ushered in a new era for Coconut Grove as the Navy built one of the nation's first naval air stations on Dinner Key, formerly an island favored by picnickers. More than 1,000 aspiring aviators trained there. Coconut Grove citizens, concerned with the noise and pollution wrought by the naval air station, brought pressure upon the federal government for its closing, which came in 1919. Soon after, Coconut Grove was incorporated as a town. In the process, it dropped the "a" from its original spelling of Cocoanut at the suggestion of world-famous horticulturist Dr. David Fairchild. The Grove remained a town for just six years, after which the onrushing City of Miami, in the midst of a great real estate boom, annexed it despite strong

opposition from Grove residents. In the meantime, the old naval air station site became host to Pan American Airways in 1929. Destined to become the world's pre-eminent airline, Pan American maintained a seaplane base there through World War II. The terminal and the picturesque seaplanes flying overhead became a huge draw for curious visitors. After the war, the Dinner Key Auditorium opened on the site of the old air base. The facility has played a wide variety of roles, hosting concerts and serving as a backdrop for various television shows. Ironically, Coconut Grove also became the center of the City of Miami's tumultuous politics after City Hall relocated in 1954 from downtown to Dinner Key.
Photo courtesy of Miami Dade Public Library System.

St. Petersburg's green benches

A 1930s view along Central Avenue of the green benches of St. Petersburg. They were a popular meeting place for residents and visitors alike. The first green benches in St. Petersburg appeared in 1908 under the supervision of Noel Mitchell, a real estate developer and salesman. The goal of this project was to provide structures on which people could comfortably socialize in the downtown area. Fond of Mitchell's idea, many around the city started to follow suit and installed their own version of the benches. Shortly following this explosion of road-side seating, the benches won national recognition when 1916 Mayor Al Lang imposed an ordinance to make all of the benches green. The benches lined the streets of St. Petersburg in long rows, and it was estimated that at their peak, there were around 7,000 of them in the city. These benches served as a charming place to socialize with friends, neighbors, and the like. According to many residents, the presence of the benches highlighted the romance of the city and symbolized hospitality. However, the well-known green benches did not hold a hospitable, romantic city image for long. The benches began to add to the profuse discrimination in St. Petersburg that was already exemplified by numerous forms of explicit and implicit racism. While no laws were implemented to restrict black residents from enjoying the benches, it was custom that police officers would only permit the white community to use them. However, black caretakers were allowed to sit on the benches while accompanying white children. Other ways of excluding the black population from St. Petersburg's city life existed but the green benches were the most prominent example. As a result, some residents believe that the green benches continue to be "an ugly symbol" of a segregationist era in history and specifically in the city of St. Petersburg.

Photo courtesy of Earl Jacobs III Collection.

Photo courtesy of the Smithsonian Institute, additional information from Historic Culture/St. Augustine Tourism.

Potato growers, Hastings, 1930s

The origin of Hastings can be traced back to Thomas Horace Hastings, a cousin of oil magnate Henry Flagler. Originally, Hastings established Prairie Garden, a 1,569-acre plantation just 18 miles west of St. Augustine, with the intention of supplying vegetables for Flagler's Hotel Ponce de Leon. At the time, the area was mostly wilderness, and the nearest railway station was in Merryfield, but Hastings wanted a station at Prairie Garden. Legend has it Mr. Hastings may have had a hand in moving the station and putting up a sign with his name on it.

The Town Charter was formed in 1909 and potatoes were the big crop, earning the title Florida's Potato Capitol. In 1917, the price of potatoes soared, which allowed locals to buy cars, jewelry, furniture, and clothes while small businesses were able to expand. Hastings played a major role in the agricultural development of Florida's east coast. Today, Hastings is the packing and shipping center for a tri-county potato growing area and continues to produce and manufacture crops for Flagler, Putnam, and St. Johns counties.

Cattle cowboys

A pair of Union County cowboys, Adam Andrews and Graham Boyd, 1930s. Hundreds of years before Florida's primary industries were citrus and tourism, cattle was king. When Ponce de León discovered Florida in 1513, he saw the wide-open green spaces, and knew that he'd found pastureland. When he returned in 1521, he brought horses and seven Andalusian cattle with him, and Spanish explorers turned Florida into America's oldest cattle-raising state. Florida's old-time cowboys used braided leather whips 10 to 12 feet long. Snapping these whips made a loud crack. That sound brought stray cattle back into line fast and earned cowboys the nickname of "crackers."

Photo courtesy of Tom Moore.

The "Florida Special"

A view inside a recreation car of the Pullman sleeping car train named the "Florida Special." This photo was taken some time in the early 1930s by Florida East Coast Railway photographer Harry M. Wolfe. Per the contributor, Seth Bramson, it is likely an Atlantic Coast Line lounge car converted to a recreation car. Pullman sleeper cars were known for their luxury and were built by the Pullman Company, founded by George Mortimer Pullman in the 1860s. The Florida Special was a long-running Atlantic Coast Line seasonal service between New York and Miami aimed at vacationers looking to escape the cold of the northeast. Its beginnings go back to 1888, when it began service as the New York & Florida Special. During World War I, it became the Florida Special and continued to operate until 1971 when Amtrak took over. *Photo courtesy of Seth Bramson.*

Great South Florida Flood

David and Mary Shropshire trying to stay dry and avoid the heavy traffic on NW 36th Street in Miami during the Great South Florida Flood of September 1947. The two-story building in the background is Dr. Harold McGee's new Veterinary Clinic at 3518 NW 36th Street. Dr. McGee had just moved his practice from Hialeah and remained at this location for many years. The McGees also lived in the building until 1951 when they moved to their new home on Hunting Lodge Drive in Miami Springs. In the span of only 25 days, two hurricanes and a tropical disturbance put 90 percent of eastern Florida from Orlando to Miami under water.

Photo courtesy of Marjorie Shropshire, daughter of David and Mary Shropshire.

Flying High Circus performance, Florida State University, Tallahassee, 1948.
Photo courtesy of May Alice Hunt/FSU Library, additional information from Florida State University.

The Flying High Circus

The Flying High Circus was created on September 1, 1947, by Jack Haskin. The goal was to create something that both men and women would be able to participate in together. The university became coed on May 15 of that same year. Since its founding, FSU's Flying High Circus has enjoyed worldwide recognition for its brilliance and creativity. The only requirement to be a member is that one must be seeking a degree at the university. The circus is primarily an aerial and stage presentation with three rings performing under a big top tent located on the campus. There are no animal acts. Student performers rig all of their own equipment, sew their own costumes, produce lights and sound for performances, and set up the big top tent on campus. The Flying High Circus recently celebrated its 75th year in existence.

Fort Myers

Emerson (Em) and Nellie Renz with their custom-made stern paddle wheel boat *Sad Sack* berthed at the Fort Myers Yacht Basin in 1949. Accompanied by their German Shepherd, they came all the way from Zanesville, Ohio, to Fort Myers, Florida, in this boat. The journey took them over three months. The route likely taken would be south from Zanesville on the Muskingum River to the Ohio River. Continuing west on the Ohio River, through Cincinnati, Ohio, and Louisville, Kentucky, until they reached the mighty Mississippi River. Southward on the Mississippi to the Gulf of Mexico, along the coasts of Mississippi and Alabama until finally reaching Florida. This route would have given them the opportunity to visit 12 different states. What a trip it must have been. *Photo courtesy of David Renz.*

Bass fishing

Julia Belle Bryant McGinness proudly displays a largemouth bass she caught in Winter Garden, 1940s. Florida has long been considered the Bass Fishing Capital of the World with its many productive bodies of water. The largemouth bass has tremendous importance to the state of Florida. It is the state fish and the backbone of the freshwater component of Florida's $5.1 billion fishing industry.

Photo courtesy of McGinness Family Archives, additional information from the Florida Museum.

Servicemen and women socializing at The Hut in West Palm Beach, 1940s.
Photo courtesy of Historical Society of Palm Beach County.

The Hut

The Hut, opened in 1930 by the Hall family and originally called The Tropical Hut, was a favorite gathering place in West Palm Beach for 43 years. There were only four seat-swiveling bar stools at the counter, so by 1937, when new owners took over, most of their business was done via curb girls who hustled out to the patio under the banyan trees, or to cars that were often parked four deep. During World War II, the neon sign drew in the servicemen and women stationed in the area. High school students would gather on Friday nights and hang out with their friends. Families would pile in the car and go for barbecue and frosted root beer. Big band music played over the jukebox; cheese dogs, fried chicken, and milkshakes were favorites on the menu.

Cocoa Beach

The McGinness Family, along with family friend Jim McRory on the right, enjoy a weekend getaway to Cocoa Beach, 1940s. There was a 1,000 percent population increase in Cocoa Beach from 1950 to 1960, mainly as a result of the U.S. space program. NASA's John F. Kennedy Space Center is located approximately 15 miles north of town. Many people moved to Cocoa Beach due to jobs connected to the space program and in search of new opportunities.

Photo courtesy of McGinness Family Archives.

Silver Springs

Visitors to Silver Springs enjoying a glass-bottom boat ride, 1940s. Although Silver Springs didn't officially open to the public until 1878, it was a popular spot for visitors years earlier when they arrived by steamboat. Silver Springs became known for its glass-bottom boat rides — thanks to the ingenuity of Hullam Jones and Phillip Monell who affixed a piece of glass to the bottom of a rowboat in the late 1870s. They were only 14 years old at the time. Due to the popularity of the boats, a countless number of souvenir photographs like this were taken over the years.

Photo courtesy of Lyn Chilton.

Gainesville in the 1940s, looking north up East Main Street (now SE 1st St.) from Union Street (now SE 1st. Ave.)

Photo courtesy of Matheson History Museum.

Gainesville

Just out of view to the left is Courthouse Square and the 1886 Alachua County Courthouse. All of the businesses on the right are now gone and the site is home to a community plaza and amphitheater named for rock and roll legend Bo Diddley. The plaza was renamed the Bo Diddley Community Plaza in 2009. Diddley performed a benefit concert there to raise money and awareness for the homeless. The singer and songwriter was a resident of nearby Archer in his later years.

Naval Air Station, Key West

The main gate to the Trumbo annex of the Naval Air Station, Key West, 1940s. Because Florida had a warm climate and a lot of vacant land available, it was ideal for building military bases. By the 1930s, Florida had 172 military installations, both large and small. Florida's position between the Atlantic Ocean and the Gulf of Mexico made it a target for enemy submarines and German U-Boats sank over 24 ships off of Florida's Atlantic and Gulf Coasts. Ships could be seen burning by Floridians and tourists. Naval stations were reactivated at Key West, Drew, and MacDill Airfields in Tampa; Elgin Field at Valparaiso; and the Pensacola Naval Air Base. By the mid 1940s, there were 40 airfields actively training military personnel throughout the state. Florida's weather conditions and flat land made it the perfect place for training, especially pilots.

Photo courtesy of Scott DeWolfe Collection/Keys Library.

Florida Highway Patrol

Florida Highway Patrolman, Key West 1950. The Florida Highway Patrol was formed by the Florida Legislature in 1939 and was authorized to hire 60 officers. Under H. Neil Kirkman, Director of the Department of Public Safety of the State of Florida, they would patrol the public highways and enforce all state laws in effect at the time. The beginning salary was $1,500 a year, and the department was funded from the sale of drivers' licenses. Uniforms were forest green, and they wore beige Stetson hats. Patrol cars had no radios until 1943. Troopers would make regular stops at service stations or grocery stores on their routes and make telephone calls for assignments or reports of wrecks.

Photo courtesy of Florida International University Library, additional information from Tampa Bay Times *and Florida Highway Patrol.*

Family fun in Daytona Beach

Dorothy McGinness sits atop Ferdinand the Bull, 1950s in Daytona Beach. The 1938 Walt Disney animated short *Ferdinand The Bull* was based on a 1936 children's book *The Story of Ferdinand* by Munro Leaf. Capitalizing on the popularity of the book and the film, an opportunistic beach photographer began snapping photos of beach goers posing on his bull shortly after the movie came out. Thousands had their photo taken with Ferdinand over the years.

Dorothy McGinness gets ready to board the *Seabreeze II* in Daytona Beach, late 1950s. The *Seabreeze II* offered two scenic cruises daily along the Halifax River. One excursion went north to the Tomoka Basin, where the Tomoka River meets the Halifax River. The highlight of this trip was a stop at Plantation Number Nine, started by Civil War veteran Chauncey Bacon who purchased the property in 1876. He planted mulberry, guava, and many varieties of citrus which were used for the production and sale of jellies, jams, and preserves. In 1909, the thriving home business was sold to M. C. Hillery, who two years later sold it to Ferdinand Nordman. Nordman opened a "jelly house" and expanded his business by selling fruit preserves via mail order. The business survived until 1968. The jelly house was demolished in 1984 to make way for a subdivision. The second *Seabreeze II* excursion was a trip south to Ponce de León Inlet and a visit to the lighthouse. The Ponce de León Light is the tallest lighthouse in Florida and the third tallest in the United States. It was built in 1835.

Photos courtesy of the McGinness family.

Blue Goose citrus packing house, Maitland

D. F. Ingram and M. R. Stover at the American Fruit Grower's Blue Goose citrus packing house in Maitland, around 1950. The packing house, located in the 100 block of George Street, opened in 1933. In the early morning of Sunday, April 27, 1969, it was destroyed by a massive fire, which is still considered the worst in the city's history. Flames and an orange glow were seen for miles. Firemen from the neighboring communities of Winter Park, Casselberry, Eatonville, Killarney and Orlando responded to assist the Maitland Fire Department in fighting the blaze. There was nothing that could be done as the building was engulfed in flames in a matter of minutes. At the time of the fire, it was no longer being used as a citrus packing plant, rather a storage facility for an insulation company.

Photo courtesy of Donna Smith.

Florida East Coast Railway Depot, Boca Raton, 1950

Built in 1930, the station was designed by F.E.C. architect Chester G. Henninger in the Mediterranean Revival style of architecture with a gently pitched gable roof, stuccoed walls, and arched loggias with delicate spiral columns. The distinctive style, generally associated with the work of Addison Mizner, contributed richly to the unique physical character of Boca Raton which remains visible today. The F.E.C. Railway Passenger Station in Boca Raton was operated until 1968 when passenger service along the line was discontinued. The station was listed on the National Register of Historic Places in 1980, and was restored in 1989. It is now home to the Boca Express Train Museum operated by the Boca Raton Historical Society.
Photo courtesy of City of Boca Raton.

Key West

President Truman is eating lunch on the lawn of the Little White House in Key West, 1951. Key West is one of Florida's most unique and interesting historic towns, and for years has been a favorite getaway for U.S. Presidents, including Harry S. Truman, Franklin D. Roosevelt, and Dwight D. Eisenhower. John F. Kennedy spent a month in the Little White House after the Cuban Missile Crisis was resolved, and Jimmy Carter had a family reunion on the property shortly after the end of his presidency. President Truman was by far the biggest Key West fan, who throughout his presidency during the late 1940s and early 1950s, made 11 visits to the island and spent a total of 175 days on vacation. Thanks to advances in technology, he was able to get plenty of work done while in Key West, and many times he called his team for meetings at the house as well as fishing trips and poker nights. His affinity for the residence spawned the nickname Truman's Little White House.

Photo courtesy of Wikimedia.

FULL SCALE
MERCURY
SPACECRAFT
MODEL

Cape Canaveral Air Force Station

NASA introduced the Project Mercury Astronauts to the world on April 9, 1959, only six months after the agency was established. Known as the Mercury 7 or Original 7, they are: Wally Schirra, Deke Slayton, John Glenn, Scott Carpenter, Alan Shepard, Gus Grissom, and Gordon Cooper. The United States was already a distant second in space technology behind the Soviet Union, who on October 4, 1957, had launched Sputnik, the world's first artificial satellite. The race to begin to explore the universe had unofficially begun. On the morning of February 20, 1962, millions of Americans collectively held their breath as roughly a hundred miles above their heads, astronaut John Glenn sat comfortably in the nine-and-a-half by six-foot space capsule he called Friendship 7, becoming the first American to orbit the Earth. With this launch, the space race was officially on, and Americans eagerly followed every launch made by NASA. The Mercury 7 astronauts quickly became heroes and celebrities.

Three young boys pose in front of a full-scale model of the Mercury 7 space capsule at Cape Canaveral Air Force Station, 1966.
Photo courtesy of Gordon Simms.

Virginia Beach Park

Children and adults line up to eagerly ride on the Virginia Beach Park miniature train, 1952. Although only accessible by boat from a downtown dock on the Miami River, Virginia Beach Park opened on August 1, 1945. Virginia Key Beach grew in popularity and it became the place to go for parties, religious gatherings, and, of course, the beach. The beach included picnic areas with barbecue pits, cottages, a boat ramp, and, as shown in the photo, the mini-train and carousel rides. Thousands flocked to Virginia Beach Park regularly. Even though the beach remained segregated throughout the 1950s, it was also enjoyed by immigrants from the Caribbean, South America, and Cuba who found the cherished getaway to be either the only beach that they too could visit, or the beach they preferred.

Photo courtesy of Virginia Key Beach Park Trust/FIU Library and Tropic Magazine.

Miami

Entertainers posing in front of FEC E6A, the Florida East Coast Railway's first diesel passenger unit, December 21, 1953, Miami.

Photo courtesy of Seth Bramson.

The performers, who were most likely chorus girls, arrived from the north to perform at Lou Walters' Latin Quarter nightclub on Palm Island, Miami Beach. Lou Walters, father of broadcast journalist and television personality Barbara Walters, was born in London as Louis Edward Waremwasser. When the family moved to New York City, they changed their surname to Walters. Young Lou got his start in the entertainment business as an office boy for a Vaudeville company. He eventually worked his way up and by his early twenties he opened his first booking agency in Boston. In 1937, he opened his first Latin Quarter nightclub in Boston with partner E. M. Lowe and it proved to be a big success. He soon opened a second Latin Quarter in Falmouth, MA. In 1940, he moved the family to Miami and opened his third location on Palm Island. The club was popular with many celebrities of the day, both as performers and guests. In 1959, the club was badly damaged in a fire and never reopened.

Ocean Terrace Motel, Juno Beach

Guests of the Ocean Terrace Motel in Juno Beach arriving by a flotilla of rental boats at Trapper Nelson's Zoo on the Loxahatchee River in 1953. The Ocean Terrace Motel was owned by the Watson family. Trapper Nelson (born Vincent Nostokovich or Natulkiewicz, 1909–1968) was a trapper and hunter. Though he was born in New Jersey, and lived in Mexico and Texas, Nelson is best known for establishing a homestead-turned-zoo on the shore of Florida's Loxahatchee River. Filled with exotic and wild animals, his zoo was a popular tourist spot in the 1940s and 1950s.

Photo courtesy of Bill Watson.

Tampa's Gasparilla celebration, 1954

Since 1905, pirates have invaded Tampa Bay. Every year, the unruly plunderers take over the city in honor of the mythical pirate Jose Gaspar. The Gasparilla Pirate Fest is one of the country's largest and most unique outdoor celebrations. It begins when the world's only fully rigged pirate ship sails into the heart of Tampa. Flanked by hundreds of pleasure craft and vessels of all shapes and sizes, the invasion is a formidable sight. Built entirely of steel, the black-hulled *Jose Gasparilla* measures 165 feet in length and is topped by three masts that tower 100 feet above deck. Tugboats tow the craft and its crew of 700 pirates, with flags flying and cannons booming, as the vessel makes its way along Hillsborough Bay. The history and name of this Tampa tradition traces back to the legendary antics of Jose Gaspar who reputedly patrolled the waters of West Florida during the late 18th century. A society columnist with the *Tampa Tribune* is credited with creating a May festival in 1904 that first incorporated a pirate-inspired theme. The original members of Ye Mystic Krewe of Gasparilla stormed Tampa on horseback before becoming seaworthy in 1911. The success of those early invasions prompted planners to move the celebration to its winter time slot and encouraged the creation of additional events.

Photo courtesy of LaMartin Collection, additional information from City of Tampa.

The Tamiami Trail

The remains of a shack along the Tamiami Trail, March 1955. The name came about by combining the city names of Tampa and Miami. It was conceived as a way to connect the two cities. The Tamiami Trail stretches more than 270 miles across Florida. It opened in the late 1920s and was considered one of the major forces in drawing tourists to the state.

Photo courtesy of Carol Vallad.

Visitors are enjoying a day on the beach, Virginia Key Beach Park, 1956.

Photo courtesy of Virginia Key Beach Park Trust/ FIU Library.

Virginia Key Beach Park

The beach was the culmination of a 25-year battle that began in 1920, which saw the development of swimming areas and parks exclusively for the white population of Miami as well as the surrounding areas. The first African American millionaire in the area, D.A. Dorsey, purchased property, which is now known as Fisher Island, so that African Americans would have their own beach to enjoy. Due to increased property taxes, Mr. Dorsey had no other choice but to sell the land which left the community without a beach to call their own. It wasn't until the 1940s that Judge Lawson E. Thomas ruled a beach on Virginia Key known as Bears Cut to be designated for the use of African Americans. The site was the response to a protest by African American men who under Thomas' leadership, defiantly entered the water with the intention of being arrested at exclusively white Baker's Haulover Beach in North Dade County. To avoid costly embarrassment, county authorities took no legal action against the protesters. Instead, they agreed to the protesters' demands for an officially designated swimming area for African Americans. Although only accessible by boat from a downtown dock on the Miami River, "Virginia Beach, a Dade County Park for the exclusive use of African Americans," was opened on August 1, 1945.

Bike Week, Daytona Beach, March 1956

Bikers gathered on Main Street in Daytona Beach during Bike Week, 1956. This view is looking east towards the Atlantic Ocean. Daytona Beach has long been a hotbed for motor sports. Drawn by the wide beaches with hard-packed sand, motorcycle and automobile makers first came here in the early 1900s to test the limits of their machines. Land speed records were set, several racers lost their lives, and in the process, Daytona Beach became synonymous with speed. On March 8, 1936, the first stock car race was held on the Daytona Beach Road Course, located in the present-day town of Ponce Inlet. Beach racing came to an end in the late 1950s when Daytona International Speedway opened. Today, you can still drive on most parts of the beach, but the speed limit is 10 miles per hour.

Bike Week, as it is known today, traces its beginnings to the inaugural running of the Daytona 200 race on January 24, 1937. It was originally just a friendly gathering of motorcycle enthusiasts who came to Daytona to attend the race. The Daytona 200 was run from 1937 to 1941 but was canceled from 1942 to 1947 because of World War II. During those years off, an unofficial gathering still took place and was commonly called Bike Week. The tradition continues to this day.

Photos courtesy of Carol Vallad.

Key West Aquarium

The Key West Aquarium was a dream of Dr. Van Deusen, a director of the Fairmount Park Aquarium in Philadelphia. Construction began during the Great Depression in 1933 as part of the Works Progress Administration Program, which helped to build many of the historic Key West attractions that inhabit the island today. This provided many jobs to local Key Westers, or Conchs as they are called today, during difficult economic times when jobs were limited and people were in need of income to support their families. The concrete that was used to form the aquarium structure and holding tanks was mixed with sea water from the ocean since fresh water was hard to come by in those days. The Aquarium took two years to complete and opened to the public on February 18, 1935. At that time, admission was 15 cents for adults and 5 cents for children. The Key West Aquarium was the first aquarium to use an open-air concept. This allowed for natural sunlight to illuminate the concrete marine displays. Dr. Van Deusen outlined the future of the Aquarium in his speech on its opening day. He stated that it was a valuable institution to biologists and students from all around the world, with hopes that it would draw thousands of people annually to Key West. The Aquarium was the island's first attraction and remains a popular one to this day.

Carol Vallad sitting on a motorcycle in front of the Key West Aquarium, February 1956.
Photo courtesy of Carol Vallad, additional information from the Key West Aquarium.

Where the Boys Are

Extras gather for direction during filming of the 1959 movie *Where the Boys Are* that starred Dolores Hart, George Hamilton, Connie Francis, and Frank Gorshin. Connie Francis is honored with a sidewalk plaque in the Fort Lauderdale Walk of Fame at A1A and Las Olas Boulevard, the location of many scenes in the movie. The Elbo Room, which is featured in the movie, is a bar that was established in 1938 at 241 South Fort Lauderdale Beach Boulevard, in Fort Lauderdale. It became a landmark for Fort Lauderdale Beach.
Photo courtesy of Gene Hyde Collection/Fort Lauderdale Historical Society.

The Goodyear blimp

The Goodyear blimp eastbound and flying low over the original MacArthur Causeway in Miami, 1950s. The bridge was replaced in the 1960s. The blimp is likely preparing to land on its base, which was located on Watson Island, now the site of Miami Children's Museum. Biscayne Island on the Venetian Causeway is in the background.

Photo courtesy of Bret Ribotsky.

Maitland

Nick Belitz's citrus packing and shipping center in Maitland, 1950s. The big orange was originally part of a fountain that was located by Lake Ivanhoe in Orlando. The fountain was constructed by the Work Projects Administration program during the Depression. It quickly became a target of criticism and graffiti artists and fell into disrepair. In 1953, Orlando city officials agreed to a plan sponsored by the Boy Scouts to build a replica of the Statue of Liberty on the site of the fountain. Citrus grower Nick Belitz acquired the ball and installed it in front of his business in Maitland. In 1983, the big orange was demolished.

Photo courtesy of Florida Roadside Attractions.

Water Ski Show at Cypress Gardens in Winter Haven, 1950s

Cypress Gardens was Florida's first theme park. It was created by entrepreneur Dick Pope, and opened on January 2, 1936. Pope was a flamboyant and successful promoter. His marketing efforts led to Cypress Gardens appearing on the covers of hundreds of magazines and in newspaper photographs across the country. The theme park became a popular setting for commercials, television shows, and films. A colorful botanical garden was the centerpiece of Cypress Gardens, but the park also featured water ski shows and boat rides. Beginning in 1940, the park became known for having Southern Belles walking the property in hoop skirts and posing for photographs. They were later joined by Spanish conquistadors and Native American girls. Aquatic film star Esther Williams, who made a popular series of swimming-based musicals in the 1940s and 1950s, was a frequent guest at the park. Williams promoted the venue with television specials. Her 1953 film *Easy to Love* was filmed at Cypress Gardens.

Before the Disney corporation built its first Florida theme park in 1971, Cypress Gardens was the most popular tourist destination in the state. While visiting Cypress Gardens prior to the construction of California's Disneyland in 1955, Roy Disney called his brother and business partner, Walt Disney, from Dick Pope's office. Roy Disney couldn't wait to tell his brother how impressed he was with Pope's theme park concept. People were happily paying good money to walk around a garden, stop for photos with costumed characters, ride in a boat, and watch entertaining shows.

Unfortunately, with the opening of Disney World and other large theme parks, revenues at Cypress Gardens began to decline. Beginning in the early 1980s, a series of new owners took control of the park, including the corporations that owned SeaWorld and Busch Gardens. In 2009, Cypress Gardens closed. Two years later, LEGOLAND Florida opened on the site. LEGOLAND features rides, shows, and a water park primarily aimed at children 12 and under. Miniature cities are constructed using the popular Lego building blocks. The original botanical gardens of Cypress Gardens are intact at the heart of the park. Even the iconic Southern Belles remain, although they are now made of Legos.

Photo courtesy of Florida News Bureau, additional information from My Florida History.

Photo courtesy of Patti Barrett.

Mobile Marine

Joe T. Barrett, taking a break in his Mobile Marine van in Orlando, 1960. He came up with the idea for this business venture while he was a partner at College Park Outboard Motors in Orlando. Customers would complain about how much of a chore it was to bring their boats or motors into the shop. He sold his interest in that business and purchased this Volkswagen van and turned it into a shop on wheels. Canadian by birth, Joe was raised in Trinidad where his father was working in the oil business. It was there that he gained a love of sailing and learned how to work on motors. He worked with his father for a while in Venezuela and it

was there that he started his first outboard motor repair business. In 1956, while en route to Canada, Joe and his wife, Esme, stopped in Orlando to see relatives and stayed. Around 1965, he opened Barrett's Marine on Fairbanks Avenue in Winter Park. A year or two later, he moved his business to Lake Fairview in Orlando where he did repairs, rented and sold sailboats, and also taught sailing. Joe later married Melinda Crenshaw. With help from Joe's kids Patti, Barry, Glen, and Jim, they operated the business for many years. Joe and Linda are currently enjoying retirement in Astor, Florida.

Jupiter Inlet Lighthouse, 1961

In 1853, Congress authorized the building of a lighthouse near Jupiter Inlet. The federal government designated a 61.5-acre lighthouse reservation the following year. However, a survey from the 1920s discovered that the reservation actually comprised 122 acres. Jupiter was one of six Florida lighthouse projects assigned to Lieutenant George Gordon Meade of the U.S. Army Corps of Topographic Engineers. A decade later, he would famously defeat Robert E. Lee at the Battle of Gettysburg as a Major General in the Union Army. Meade selected the site and created the original design for the Jupiter Inlet Lighthouse. His successor, Lieutenant William F. Raynolds, improved on the final design by adding height and a double wall. Edward A. Yorke, a civilian, oversaw construction of the light station in 1859 and 1860. Today, the Jupiter Inlet Lighthouse & Museum is operated by the Loxahatchee River Historical Society.

Photo courtesy of Historical Society of Palm Beach County,

John Glenn

President John F. Kennedy, astronaut John Glenn and General Leighton I. Davis (in back seat, from left to right) ride together during a parade in Cocoa Beach after Glenn's historic February 20, 1962, spaceflight in which he became the first U.S. citizen to orbit the earth. Glenn orbited the earth three times in his space capsule Friendship 7, reaching speeds of over 17,000 miles per hour. The flight lasted just under five hours. Overnight, Glenn became a national hero and a household name. Ironically, when Glenn lifted off in Friendship 7, his backup, Scott Carpenter, spoke the same words from mission control that were used in NASA's announcement of his death: "Godspeed, John Glenn."

Photo courtesy of PICRYL, additional information from NASA and Wikimedia Commons.

Liftoff of the Mercury Atlas 9 spacecraft at 8:04 AM EST, May 15, 1963.
Photo and information courtesy of NASA.

Mercury Atlas 9

Mercury Atlas 9 (MA-9, designated also Faith 7) was the fourth and final manned orbital flight of the Mercury program. The pilot was L. Gordon Cooper, Jr. The objectives of MA-9 were to: (1) evaluate the effects on the astronaut of approximately one day in orbital flight; (2) verify that man can function for an extended period in space as a primary operating system of the spacecraft; and, (3) evaluate in a manned, one-day mission the combined performance of the astronaut and a Mercury spacecraft specifically modified for the mission.

Originally scheduled for launch in April, the mission was delayed twice. The first delay (February) was due to a decision to rewire the Mercury-Atlas flight control system. The second (May 14) occurred on the scheduled day of launch when a problem developed with the fuel pump in the diesel engine used to retract the gantry from the launch vehicle. This resulted in a delay of roughly 129 minutes after countdown had already reached T-60 minutes. Subsequent to the repairs on the gantry engine, the failure of a computer converter at the Bermuda tracking station forced a further cancellation of the launch at T-13 minutes. The launch was rescheduled for the following day (May 15).

The countdown then proceeded without a hitch until T-11 minutes and 30 seconds when a problem developed in the guidance equipment and a brief hold was called until it was resolved. Another hold was called at the T-19 second mark to ascertain whether the systems had gone into automatic sequencing as planned. The liftoff ended up being excellent, with flight sequencing (booster engine cut-off, escape tower jettison, sustainer engine cut-off) operating perfectly and the spacecraft being inserted into orbit at a velocity described as being "almost unbelievably correct."

Lyndon B. Johnson campaigning in Orlando, October, 1964

The Cadillac Limo is traveling west on Central Boulevard in front of the old Chamber of Commerce building. The motorcade, which began at the Cherry Plaza Hotel by Lake Eola, traveled west on Central Boulevard, north on Orange Avenue, and then east on Colonial Drive to the Colonial Plaza Mall, where a huge, fenced parking lot allowed for a crowd of 40,000 residents to greet him. This trip marked the first time a sitting president had visited Orlando. This car was the Secret Service car that was directly behind John F. Kennedy's limo when he was assassinated in Dallas on November 22, 1963. Johnson's presidential limo had yet to be built.

Photo courtesy of the LBJ Presidential Library, additional information from Doug Head and Dick Camnitz.

The Beatles

The Beatles arrived at Jacksonville's Imeson Airport on their first American tour, September 1964. A few days prior to their scheduled performance at the Gator Bowl Stadium, they learned the concert was going to be racially segregated. They refused to perform until they received an assurance from the promoter that the audience would be mixed. John Lennon said: "We never play to segregated audiences and we aren't going to start now. I'd sooner lose our appearance money."

Officials eventually relented and the show went on desegregated, a first for Jacksonville. The band was so appalled, they had it written into their contract that the audiences of future shows would be allowed to sit wherever they'd like. The concert was also notable because it was held the day after Hurricane Dora struck St. Augustine and Jacksonville. Most of Jacksonville was without electricity and power was not restored for several days. Despite the hurricane, 23,000 fans attended, paying four and five dollars for tickets. During the concert, Ringo Starr's drums were nailed to the stage because of 45 mph winds.

Photo courtesy of Florida Times-Union.

Friendship Fountain, Jacksonville

When it opened in 1965, the Friendship Fountain in Jacksonville was the world's largest and tallest fountain. It was designed by Jacksonville architect Taylor Hardwick. Its three pumps could push 17,000 gallons of water per minute up to 100 feet in height. The 14-acre Friendship Park was donated by the Southside Business Men's Club.

Photo by Leo Witt, courtesy of the Jacksonville Historical Society.

Amaryllis

The Greek cargo ship *Amaryllis* ran aground in the shallows off Singer Island at Palm Shores, 1966. On September 7, 1965, as Hurricane Betsy approached Florida, *Amaryllis,* bound from Manchester, England, to Baton Rouge, Louisiana, sought refuge in the Port of Palm Beach. Sometime during the night, as she approached the Palm Beach Inlet, steering problems along with high winds forced her into the shallow waters and coral reefs north of the inlet. The ship became an attraction for sightseers and surfers who found the ship to be one of the most spectacular surf spots in the area. It took over three years before the ship was finally removed from the beach. Wrecking crews took it apart piece by piece and the remains were sunk in 100 feet of water off the Palm Beach Inlet to serve as an artificial reef.

Photo courtesy of Digital Public Library of America.

The Boardwalk, Daytona Beach, 1969

The Boardwalk was installed in the late 1920s; the bandshell and the surrounding areas were completed in 1939. It was initially called the Broadwalk because of the width of the walkway and the fact that it is made out of cement rather than wood. The editor of the local newspaper refused to call it the Broadwalk in print, because of the negative connotation of the word broad. For that reason alone, the common name has since become the Boardwalk. In 1985, Fort Lauderdale decided to change their image to a more family-friendly vacation spot, so with the help of MTV in 1986, Spring Break made its way to Daytona Beach, bringing crowds to the boardwalk that far exceeded Bike Week. Eventually the town's police, fire, and health officials, spurred on by city council members, began to move in the same direction as Fort Lauderdale. By 1993, MTV picked up their cameras and left Daytona Beach behind. Today Daytona Beach is still a Spring Break destination but not to the extent it was back in the 1980s.

Photo courtesy of Digital Commonwealth, additional information from Vogue and Orlando Weekly.

De Soto Plaza and Fountain

Built in 1925, the fountain is named after Spanish explorer Hernando de Soto. The plaza features a monumental free-standing fountain that serves as a traffic circle at the intersection of Sevilla Avenue, Granada Boulevard, and De Soto Boulevard. Designed by Denman Fink, the pedestal-type fountain supports an obelisk and features four relief carvings of faces containing water jets. Vintage lanterns provide light when the dark of night falls. The design is considered to be neobaroque, a French architectural style of the late 19th century.

The De Soto Plaza and Fountain in Coral Gables in the early 1960s.
Photo courtesy of Coral Gables Memory, additional information from Ashley Cusack.

Aloha Lagoon, Cape Coral

Many television commercials and movies were filmed at the Aloha Lagoon. It featured wild peacocks, goldfish, waterfalls, and tiki torches. The tropical foliage was considered the finest in all of Southwest Florida.

Aloha Lagoon at Cape Coral Gardens in the town of Cape Coral, 1970.
Photo courtesy of Cape Coral Historical Society.

The Magic Kingdom

Roy O. Disney is delivering an opening-day speech on October 1, 1971, at the Magic Kingdom in Walt Disney World.

When Walt Disney died on December 15, 1966, Roy O. Disney saw his brother's dream to completion. He was as much responsible for the creation and success of Walt Disney World as was his younger brother, founder and namesake, Walter E. Disney. Originally, the park was going to be called "Disney World." It was Roy's idea to call the park "Walt Disney World" to honor his brother. On October 1, 1971, Walt Disney World Magic Kingdom opened to a crowd of 10,000 guests with 23 rides and attractions. Over the next few months, several more attractions were added. Disney now operates four parks near Orlando including the original Disney's Magic Kingdom Park, Disney's Animal Kingdom Park, Disney's Hollywood Studios, and Epcot. Combined, they attract approximately 57,000 guests daily. Walt Disney World recently celebrated its 50th anniversary in Florida, and its impact to the state has been felt in all areas of life.

Photo courtesy of Disney Archives, Orlando Sentinel.

Channel TV

Channel TV opened in May of 1968. Today, it would be considered a throwback. Channel TV, along with other merchants on the block, were considered mom-and-pop stores — independent businesses where shopkeepers knew your name and were eager to help you.

Channel TV and Electronics truck #4, 911 Normandy Drive, Miami Beach, 1972.

Photo courtesy of Davies Family Archives.

The Dolphin Show at the Miami Seaquarium, 1976

In 1954, Fred Coppock and Captain W.B. Gray opened the Seaquarium in Miami. It quickly became one of South Florida's most popular attractions. In the 1960s, the popular television show *Flipper* filmed many episodes at the Seaquarium along with two movies. Over 500,000 people visit each year. Until 1991, the Seaquarium had its own version of the monorail which it called the Spacerail.

Photo courtesy of Bret Ribotsky.

The Desert Inn at Yeehaw Junction, late 1970s

As early as 1889, the Desert Inn, located at the intersection of SR 60 and US 441 known as Yeehaw Junction, was a bar room and brothel for cowboys and lumber workers. It was originally named Jackass Crossing, a reference to the burros that ranchers rode to the inn. Throughout the years, it was used as a trading post, hotel, restaurant, gas station, and dance hall. In 1994, it was added to the National Register of Historic Places.

The Desert Inn closed in the summer of 2018 and was in the process of cleanup and restoration when, in the early morning hours of December 22, 2019, a tractor trailer crashed into the side of the inn. The building was severely damaged and according to the Osceola County Historical Society, which owns the property, it may have to be demolished.

Photo courtesy of Toasy Martin.

Jantzen Red Diving Girl

Seen here in the late 1970s, the iconic Jantzen Red Diving Girl soared above Stamie's Smart Beachwear Shop on Ocean Avenue in Daytona Beach since the mid 1960s. In 2017, the swimwear shop closed and Jantzen wanted its girl back. She is one of only four fiberglass mannequins still in existence. So she was shipped off to storage in Washington State. Her departure drew a backlash from a community who had fallen in love with her over the years. Perry Ellis International, the company that now owns Jantzen, noticed the outcry. Before they agreed to send her back, they wanted to ensure that Daytona Beach and Volusia County would have an appropriate, safe place for her to come back to, after a restoration. That's when International Speedway Corporation stepped up and offered a permanent home near the splash park at One Daytona. And just like that, the city's beloved diver in red came home.

Photo courtesy of Toasy Martin, additional information from Cassidy Alexander.